Prison Life and Human Worth

*Published with assistance from
the Roger E. Joseph Memorial Fund
for greater understanding of
public affairs, a cause in which
Roger Joseph believed*

Prison Life and Human Worth

by PAUL W. KEVE

UNIVERSITY OF MINNESOTA
PRESS □ MINNEAPOLIS

365.973
K43p

Library of Congress Catalog Card Number: 74-84252
ISBN 0-8166-0734-6

Preface

IT IS GOOD to note that the United States public is more concerned today than ever before about its correctional system and perhaps is beginning to realize the bewildering complexity of the challenge it presents. Having in mind both the complexity and the public concern, I thought that one more book might well be ventured in the interest of adding my own modest views to the uncertain light being shed from many sources on this intriguing social problem. There is need to tell in simple and human terms what happens to people — both the guards and the guarded — in prison. So this book speaks particularly to those who anxiously urge that prisons be administered with more corrective effect and order, but who do not know that the prison can guarantee neither correction of its inmates nor their orderliness, no matter how qualified the administrators.

My own direct observations through many years of corrections work are augmented here by the privilege I have had of visiting institutions throughout this country and abroad, and of engaging in countless sessions of shop talk with other corrections administrators, rank and file staff members, inmates, former inmates, and other thoughtful observers.

v

I am keenly conscious that the tone of my message is, in places, sharply critical of correctional institutions, and this may disappoint some of my friends in this work. At the same time, for every person who winces at the words of criticism there will be not just one but probably many who will earnestly protest that I am too charitable. This results in part from the problem of having to describe in general terms a system that is so exceedingly diverse that anything at all can be said about it and still be correct for some segment of it somewhere.

My focus here is not the entire correctional system, but only its most visible element — the massive, traditional custodial institution. Though there are now some small, open, and much improved institutions, only a fraction of the incarcerated offenders are in such new facilities, and even the newest and best of these are not altogether free of some of the problems described here. But I am arbitrarily limiting most of this discussion to the great walled prisons, for they easily present problems enough for one book. They house tens of thousands of men and women — and sometimes children — causing perpetual damage to their inmates with utterly unproductive expense to us all.

The occasional anecdotal illustrations used here are true as recounted except that inmate names are changed.

Obviously this kind of presentation can be prepared only with the willingness of many people to contribute viewpoints and criticisms, and with the generosity of prison administrators in permitting my free discussions with staff and inmates.

There are so many of them. My sincerest thanks to every one.

Paul W. Keve

Contents

Prison Life and Human Worth

> . . . *our prison system is a*
> *horrible accidental growth and*
> *not a deliberate human invention,*
> *and its worst features have been*
> *produced with the intention, not*
> *of making it worse, but of making*
> *it better.*
>
> George Bernard Shaw

CHAPTER 1

Prison: The Well-Intentioned
Accident

LET THERE be no mistake about it. We need prisons.

Until some distant day when we develop techniques that are thus far unknown, we will have to provide safekeeping for those few misfits who are truly dangerous and whose problems do not yield to any artistry presently available to us.

But for the majority of those prisoners who are in our institutions right now, we must have something drastically different from the traditional prison, and quickly.

The public feels, mostly at a visceral level, that the threat of imprisonment is a necessary deterrent to crime, and periodically the feeling becomes rampant that judges are not locking up enough people for long enough periods of time. The problem was typified by the appearance one day outside the Criminal Courts Building in St. Louis of a lone housewife who was picketing the court with a large poster which asked, "When are the courts going to stop turning loose criminals to endanger our lives?" She was just an average housewife from the St. Louis suburbs who made her own decision to picket the courthouse after a young woman had been murdered in a shopping center parking lot in that area a few days previously. The culprit was not yet known so the picketing housewife was only making an angry supposition that the recent crime was committed by someone who was at large by courtesy of a lenient court. The lady's anger and frustration were entirely understandable, and her demand that something be done to remedy the situation was entirely justified. The only thing wrong was the naïveté of the solution she sought — the locking up of more people for more time.

That picketing in St. Louis occurred just two weeks after three inmates and three guards had died violently in San Quentin Prison and a few days before the awful rebellion at the Correctional Facility, Attica, New York, which took the lives of thirty-two inmates and ten staff. But even the total of forty-eight deaths in the short span of less than four weeks could not fully define the scope of these two tragedies. For extending in every direction from the bloodied cell block floors of San Quentin and Attica were the devastating reactionary echoes of fear, bitterness, distrust, and the old calls for return to harsh control and repression. In those two prisons as in all others in the land, recent years have brought efforts to treat men more humanely — more softly, the critics call it. Instantly the assumption arises after a riot that we have gone too far with softness; that the permissiveness of today's prison administrators has led to this trouble, and back we must hasten to the sensible, strict control of earlier days.[1]

How badly our memories serve us!

We have always had prison disturbances. Before the Attica riot there had never been such large numbers of men killed in a single disturbance (except when inmates started a fire in a rebellion at the Ohio State Penitentiary in 1930, resulting in the death of 317 inmates), but violent rebellions have periodically occurred and always with potential for multiple deaths. Clinton Prison at Dannemora, New York, certainly earned repute as a strict and no-nonsense prison, but in 1929 three prisoners were killed there in a riot. A week later another New York prison, Auburn, erupted with resultant deaths of two inmates and three guards. Three months later

---

[1] "The residents [of Attica] feel strongly that the riot occurred because of the 'permissiveness' of state officials — notably Oswald, who is as heartily detested as the inmates." *Time*, September 27, 1971, p. 23.

seven guards were killed in an escape attempt by Colorado Prison inmates. In 1912 a riot by 1000 inmates at the Nebraska Penitentiary caused the deaths of two staff and three inmates. At California's Folsom Prison nine inmates and three guards were killed in a 1927 rebellion.

These are only a few among many fatal prison disturbances which occurred in prisons that were never accused of coddling prisoners. So we have riots when we are hard and tough; we have riots when we try to be more relaxed and humane. It is no wonder that the public is frustrated and confused about what should be done, and asks desperately when the government is going to get these prisons under control and stop these outrageous disturbances.

The answer is simple and dismaying. Never.

As long as we have massive prisons like those we depend on today, we will have periodic violence in them just as we have had from their beginning. And the violence is going to become more frequent and more serious. This is not because we are replacing the old heavy-handed approach with something more gentle. The riots will come either way, for the prison, whatever the quality of its management, imposes a life that is deeply at odds with basic human needs. Any prisoner who reaches with persistence for those same values of freedom, creativity, and personal fulfillment which America is all about will find himself in direct collision with the prison regimen which cannot tolerate these virtues, for they jeopardize the measures of control that are necessary to the secure confinement of one or two thousand men in one tight complex.

This brings us to the searing thought that perhaps the recurring prison rebellions are in fact an awesome sign of health among frustrated people who no longer are tolerant of such prodigious defeat as they suffer in the typical prison. It is a thought that will seem warped and absurd to the beleaguered warden, and it is a thought that will seem downright obscene to the widow whose husband died as a hostage after thankless years of low-paying guard service. But we all have the tendency to assess prison disturbances in immediate and even cursory terms. This is typified by the fairly superficial reasons prisoners have usually given for their rebellions, until the more recent instances. The real reasons for riots are very fundamental, but because they are subjective and hard to define in terms of demands they have not usually been specified, if indeed understood by the prisoners themselves.

However, today's leaders in prison rebellions understand the basic issue with much more sophistication than has been evident in the past, and the high casualty list at Attica was a direct result of this new perceptiveness. Julian Tepper and Tony Fitch of the "Observers Committee," which attempted to mediate with prisoners during the Attica revolt, described the first meeting with convict representatives. "During this time there is remarkably little profanity. Most important of all, the inmates stress again and again their desire for respect. 'We will be treated as human beings,' one pleads. Another, near tears, swears that 'we will live like people or die like men.'"[2]

We should not be surprised to learn that prisoners yearn to be treated as human beings. All around us the ghetto streets have periodically burst with violent indignation at the demeaning inequities suffered by the have-nots. If we listen closely to what the ghetto rioters are saying, we find that they are not just angered by their lack of jobs and income, but angered more by those societal conditions and attitudes which frustrate their efforts to improve their lot and enhance their dignity.

When such people come into our prisons they find there a microcosm of the ghetto's frustrations, denied opportunities, and purposeless living. To bring this explosive potential to a critical point needs only the right leadership and the right incident for a spark. The leadership has been lacking or effectively suppressed in the past, but it is increasingly emerging among today's more politically sophisticated prisoners.

The revolutionary leader in prison is a devastating problem to his custodians because he has a clear and single-minded dedication to what in his view is a well-defined goal, while the prison system which holds him has far less self-assurance. No matter how clear the resolve or how humane the instincts of the warden, his operation reflects the

---

[2] *Washington Post*, September 19, 1971, p. A18.

varying philosophies of corrections people, of legislators, and of their tax-paying constituents. The militant prisoner knows exactly what he wants, whereas the rest of us must yet decide what the purpose of a prison is and how to shape it to serve that purpose.

We have very little time, for today's prisoners are challenging the correctional system in a manner so ominous that either states must institute processes of change with great rapidity or else change will be forced with recurring bloodbaths.

What Is the Prison For?

The first, but least often mentioned, purpose of prison probably is revenge. The purpose most often mentioned is deterrence, and included in this concept is the highly advertised concern for protecting the public. A third purpose (mentioned quite frequently, but a bit apologetically) is treatment of the offender.

The idea of revenge is nowhere official and almost no one will admit to its being a proper concern, for we all recognize the primitive and unworthy character of vengefulness. And yet any thoughtful observation of our handling of offenders makes it clear that underlying our legal formalities there is a need for revenge which shows itself in our emphasis upon penal time. Both the courts and the parole boards are constantly aware of this when sentencing or acting upon requests for parole, for they know that the public demands the serving of time; the more serious the offense, the more time to be served.

To avoid admitting the revenge motive we tell ourselves that it is a matter of deterrence. But the public consistently refuses to look at and act on the evidence regarding deterrence. Just why is it that correctional institutions are so popularly supported for their deterrent value when their failure in this respect has been so persistently publicized? The reason is clear and simple: prisons are supported by well-adjusted and law-abiding citizens who make the mistake of assuming that their own reaction to the threat of imprisonment is not essentially different from that of the offender.

Why is it that the thought of going to jail is abhorrent to the average person? It is not that he fears physical discomfort. He can go roughing it on a camping trip and have a wonderful time even though both the food and the mattress may be worse than a good jail would provide. Nor is the sheer threat of confinement any great concern in itself. No, the average law-abiding man is abhorrent of jail because by going there he would lose too much. He has a good job or good career prospects that would be jeopardized by a jail record. He enjoys the affection and respect of parents, wife, children, friends, and associates. Just as important, he enjoys his own self-respect, and none of these important emotional satisfactions does he want to reduce by getting a record as a jailbird. In other words, it is mainly the *stigmatic* potential of jail that gives it a deterrent effect for Mr. Average Man. But this is quite enough. In fact, it means that the threat of jail is a powerful deterrent force to the well-adjusted and law-abiding man or woman. Unfortunately, as a voter and taxpayer he supports this crime control concept based on his own personal reaction to penal sanctions, and he fails to consider the man who has never had any of these personal advantages to lose.

Many of our jail inmates have known the world of jails from their earliest experiences. Their parents, their friends, and even they themselves as children were occasionally in jail. They grew up among people who do not look down on friends who go to jail. In some situations it even confers a bit of status. They have no career expectations that are jeopardized by jail. They work at jobs that are casually obtained with no questions asked about arrest records. Such a person knows that he can commit a dozen or so burglaries and perhaps get caught once. If he is sent to prison for a term, well, he has made a living from his burglaries and now the state will provide his living for a while. When he comes out he is about where he would have been if he had not been sent away. In the culture in which he lives he is not stigmatized. He never had high self-esteem or any ambition for the kind of life style that would be hurt by a jail record.

The Illusion of Deterrence

In late 1973 a significant document on correctional problems was issued by the U.S. government. *The Report on Corrections*, produced by the National Advisory Commission on Criminal Justice

Standards and Goals, represents the carefully considered conclusions of the country's most respected thinkers on this subject. They make their position clear on the illusion of deterrent value in imprisonment.

The deterrence of potential offenders has not been supported by evidence. Despite many attempts, especially in the controversies over capital punishment, no one has ever proved that the threat of severe punishment actually deters crime. Indeed, there is evidence that swiftness and certainty have much greater deterrent effect than a long prison sentence. . . .

Documentation of the foregoing is available, particularly with reference to the failure of imprisonment in primary deterrence; that is, the discouragement of further criminal activity by those punished at least once (p. 224).

In today's social context there is a factor which is new to the conventional civilian prison. Prisoners of war never have felt stigmatized by their experience. In fact, the prisoner of war often enjoys a heroic aura following his rescue and return to civilian life. And now, whether or not the great middle-class public sees it that way, the revolutionary prisoner views himself every bit as much as a prisoner of war and enjoys the respect of his friends who support what they believe to be his fight against the repressive establishment. Prison has not a shred of deterrent value against such a man, nor does the threat of death in a prison uprising, as Attica amply showed.

The legislator who appropriates money for bigger prisons and the voters who keep him in office define deterrence in terms of their own psychology and rarely consider the fact that the kind of thing that helps to keep them honest has no effect on those people who go to penal institutions. Indeed, the prison defeats its own purposes in this respect. For if a person does have something to lose and is somewhat deterred by the threat of prison, he no longer has this advantage after his first trip to that place. Any career expectations and self-respect he might have had are undermined by his first prison experience. Furthermore, his fear of prison life is removed because he has been there, he has proved he can survive it, and he knows the tricks of getting along if he must go back again. So the prison itself conditions men to be undeterred by it, and the only people who do not know this are those who have not been there.

Occasionally some evidence is produced that supports public belief in prison as a deterrent. It is claimed, for instance, that severe and consistent use of jail sentences for drunk drivers has effectively reduced this offense. If so, it still does not prove the deterrent value of prison for offenders in general, for the majority of persons who try to drive home after one too many are not the habitual criminals who have little regard for stigma, but are middle-class persons who have not been to jail and very much want to avoid it. So admittedly they will be deterred by threat of prison.

⌈Of course, a major part of the argument in favor of prison as a deterrent is expressed as a concern for protecting the public.⌉ It is a serious and important concern, and perhaps more imprisonment would be justified if prisons actually were of any great use in protecting the public. But if they do not protect us by scaring potential offenders into being good, the only part of the public protection argument we have left is that at least while a man is in prison he is not being a threat to the outside community. The argument is more comforting than it deserves to be.

Consider the fact that convicted male felons remain in prison an average of two or three years, varying a bit from state to state. Most prisoners are relatively young men when first sentenced; if a man goes to prison at the age of nineteen, for instance, he will be coming out by the age of twenty-two in most cases. He is still young, energetic, and impulsive. In all probability his prison experience has caused him to resent the world even more than he had before, and he is now ready to make up for lost time. His two or three years' imprisonment has been only a gesture on the part of society toward its own protection. In fact, in long-range terms we may have defeated the purpose completely.

A natural response to this will be that we should take care of the problem with longer sentences. Three years as an average for time served is much too short anyway. Courts are too lenient. Lengthen the sentences.

Much of the answer to this lies in the message of the succeeding chapters, but let us look at the issue here just to the extent of some simple arithmetic. Assume we have a prison with a capacity of 1500, a fairly typical size in this country. If the average time served is three years, then this prison, provided its population figure remains fairly stable, is discharging about 500 prisoners each year and receiving new ones at the same rate. Now suppose in the interests of public protection we could suddenly double the time served, protecting the community from each man for six years instead of just three. The result would be that the institution population would no longer fit its capacity of 1500, but would double to 3000. Costs to the taxpayer would go up, and the crowded housing would cause more trouble in the prison, more likelihood of costly disturbances, more certainty of the deterioration of individuals that leads to new trouble after release. And that prisoner who was going to come out at age twenty-two will now come out at age twenty-five, still young and still more hostile.

Some prisons now have low populations and could tolerate an increase in prisoner time, but many prisons are at capacity and others are operating with gross overcrowding. New ones can be built, of course, but in 1971 the cost of security prison construction was running about 30,000 dollars or more per bed. A prison was costing about double the amount per square foot of a typical secondary school building.

Furthermore, a prison must be operated around the clock, every day of the year, and this is a high and inexorable drain on tax dollars. In Minnesota it was calculated that the cost of sending a young man to the state reformatory for one year was slightly higher than the cost of sending a student to Harvard for a year. With costs like these we had better be very sure that we truly will get some protection before we get casual about resorting to the simplistic expedient of more jail time.

Despite all this it must be admitted that there is a type of case in which the prison does serve as a protection to the public, and that is in respect to the custody of those men who need to be held for very long sentences because of severe assaultiveness that cannot otherwise be controlled. Even in these cases it often appears that the roots of these prisoners' bitter estrangement from society go back to the handling they received in earlier incarcerations; that if somehow they could have been kept out of correctional facilities from the beginning they might now be far more tolerable in the community. Of course, this cannot possibly justify releasing them in a dangerous condition now, but it lends still more urgency to the quest for something better than prison for the newer offender.[3]

To conjure up an illustration of the problem, consider a typical prison case — the young man who is sentenced for an attempted rape. Recognizing the inherent danger in generalizing, we may, nevertheless, presume certain characteristics to be found in this offender. In the first place he has the same needs that every normal male has — to be sure of his masculine identity; to be competent in his masculinity by being a husband, father, breadwinner, head of family. He also has a need just to be an individual, a person with his own uniqueness. We all like to be individual, each with his own choice of employment, hobbies, clothes, automobile, house, etc., etc. A secure sense of masculinity and a secure sense of individuality are twin needs of every man, and the satisfaction of such needs is one of the vital factors that keep us functioning as normal social beings.

What then is the problem with our young would-be rapist? Certainly it is not a problem of excess sexual drive. Probably in the physical sense he is relatively normal, but he is likely to have real doubts about his masculinity, his competence, his worth as an individual. In short, a clinical appraisal would suggest that proper treatment in his case would call for a skilled effort to build up his confidence in himself; to guide him in socially acceptable ways to prove to himself his own masculinity and uniqueness so that he will not again have to resort to such an offensive means of self-assertion.

But the court, responding more to traditional demands than to clinical indicators, commits the young man to prison to "teach him a lesson," and everything that happens to him there goes directly

---

[3] For a perceptive account of how one man's criminal career was directly fostered by his experience in training schools and reformatories, see *Killer*, by Thomas E. Gaddis and James O. Long (New York: Macmillan, 1970).

contrary to his needs. Instead of helping him achieve a self-image of competent masculinity, his new situation immediately deprives him of any opportunity to assume the traditional masculine role. Someone else must support his family and be a parent to his children. Another real fear often is that someone else will be bed partner to his wife.

Where he needs assurance that he is a unique individual, our prison proceeds to discourage uniqueness in every way. He is given a haircut and a uniform like everyone else. He is put into a cell that duplicates hundreds of others in the same cell block. He is deprived of decision-making opportunities. Someone else decides what he will eat and when he will eat it; where he will work; what his recreation will be; what time he will rise and go to bed.

If we tried to design a regimen for him that would guarantee a reversal of everything that is needed for his help and correction, we could hardly do better than to resort to the conventional prison.

For a different type of offender and from a somewhat different rationale the same argument is advanced by a researcher who reports on a study of shoplifters in the Chicago area. "Not having the support of a criminal subculture, pilferers are very 'reformable' individuals. If the findings of this study are substantiated by studies of other offenses in which the offenders are similarly without support of a criminal subculture, there would be strong argument in favor of keeping pilferers out of jail lest they receive there the kinds of knowledge and emotional support to become 'successful' commercial thieves. Crime prevention would seem best achieved by helping the law violators retain their self-image of respectability while making it clear to them that a second offense will really mean disgrace."[4]

Of course the most popular argument for keeping persons, especially first offenders, out of prison comes from the concern that the new prisoner will be schooled in the techniques of crime by the "hardened" criminals he meets there and will for this reason emerge as a more criminally conditioned ex-convict. Undoubtedly it sometimes happens, but in reality this is an insignificant aspect of the

---

[4] Mary Owen Cameron, in *Criminal Behavior Systems*, ed. Marshall B. Clinard and Richard Quinney (New York: Holt, Rinehart and Winston, 1967), p. 118.

whole criminalization problem. The far more devastating effect is found in the loss of self-esteem and the related loss of motivation that prison life induces.

The effectiveness of the prison as a school for crime is exaggerated, for the criminal can learn the technology of crime far better on the streets. The damage the prison does is more subtle. Attitudes are brutalized, and self-confidence is lost. The prison is a place of coercion where compliance is obtained by force. The typical response to coercion is alienation, which may take the form of active hostility to all social controls or later a passive withdrawal into alcoholism, drug addiction, or dependency.[5]

Even with arguments like these and with abundant evidence of prisons' failures to reform, the public is terribly reluctant to yield its trust in punishment and would prefer, with its support of rehabilitation programs in prisons, to impose both punishment and treatment at the same time. But we must seriously face and effectively answer the question whether a person can ever be helped by anything we do for him in a setting that by its every inherent characteristic is so inimical to his needs.

[5] *The Report on Corrections*, the National Advisory Commission on Criminal Justice Standards and Goals, p. 223.

CHAPTER 2

The Quality of Prison Life

THERE IS a slang phrase which probably originated far from any prison but which applies better to prison life than do any other two words in the English language — "put-down." It eloquently describes the emotional effect of being squelched, and as a noun it tells sadly, bitterly just what prison is. To the person who never has served time it is hard to realize just how much of a daily humiliating "put-down" prison life can be even in a well-run institution.

It isn't necessary to have a callous or inept warden to have a riot. It isn't necessary to have sadistic guards, bad food, or any of the other classic grievances that supposedly provoke a riot. Those will be only surface complaints. The real problem is that even in a prison with good food and humane custodians life is still a put-down, day after day after day. Boredom, pettiness, and repetitive meaningless activities are inherent in prison existence, and it should be no surprise that at some point the inmate population has had all it can stand.

The more acid-tongued critics of prisons would have us believe that the reasons for the degrading treatment of convicts lie with prison administrators who are politically motivated and unfeeling in their neglect or exploitation of prisoners. It is true enough that there have been such, and in a way it would sometimes be better if the mistreatment of prisoners was always the direct and specific mischief of an irresponsible warden. Then it becomes a problem that can be attacked. An example would be the conviction of former warden Tom Bruton in 1970 for cruel treatment of his prisoners at Arkansas' Tucker Prison Farm.

The more severe problem, however, is just the everyday put-down in the average prison where the harried warden does the best he can and prides himself on being honest and fair. Even then the prison is a severe depressant of the human spirit, and this in its long-term effects may be more damaging to the inmates than occasional physical abuse would be. "Suffering within the penal system has not decreased. The opposite seems to be the case: rehabilitation has introduced a new form of brutality, more subtle and elusive."[1] When abuse becomes psychological instead of physical, when it is supplied by well-intentioned persons who do not mean to abuse, it is then in its worst form for it does not appear to the public as evil and so it is not made the subject of investigation and ameliorative effort. At the same time those prisoners who rebel against it have difficulty in articulating their complaints and the public is more certain of their unworthiness for having rebelled against an apparently benign administration. Still, a good warden knows he is running a facility that is basically defective in concept, obsolete, and impossible to govern with equity and helpfulness to all its inmates. Yet it exists, and the warden sticks with it because someone must run it until society comes up with a better idea.

Whether or not the warden knows what that better way is, one thing he does know with certainty is that the prison must be run within the budget provided, and this inevitably means boredom and regimentation. People may not agree on the finer philosophical concepts of the purpose of a prison, but they have to agree, usually very sadly, that in the face of budgetary realities the first considerations are economy of operation and convenience of staff.

[1] *Struggle for Justice: A Report of Crime and Punishment in America*, prepared for the American Friends Service Committee (New York: Hill and Wang, 1971), p. 96.

Outnumbered Staff

Operating with a first consideration for economy and convenience is not necessarily blindness or insensitivity on the part of the warden, although it easily can lead in time to a blunting of his sensibilities. Mainly, it is a hard reality of governmental operation. In the Minnesota State Prison, for instance, the size of the staff has not been the best, but it is far from the worst among prisons. The total there in 1968 of about 280 staff for an inmate population of 900 to 1000 sounds generous to legislators who are pressured from all sides for more money than they can possibly find in their revenues. But of those 280 staff members, many would be in office, maintenance, or shop work and not available for the guarding or direct supervisory or counseling work with inmates. Add to this the usual rule of thumb that it requires about four and a half full-time staff positions to keep just one man on duty at a post around the clock. (At three shifts per day there are twenty-one shifts per week. One man works five shifts weekly, so four men can cover twenty of the twenty-one shifts. About one additional half-time person is required for the remaining shift and to cover throughout the year the holidays, sick leave, and vacation leave of the other four men.)

The result is that the Minnesota Prison had a grand total of twenty-eight men on duty on a typical evening shift. This meant that during that peak activity period of the day when men were out of their cells and engaged in recreational programs, only twenty-eight guards were on hand to control nearly a thousand prisoners. And these twenty-eight men had to be distributed between front gate, wall towers, power plant, segregation cell block, main cell blocks, hospital, school rooms, recreation yard, gymnasium. During the late night shift the staff complement dropped to a mere eighteen men.

The consequence of this is that the movement and control of masses of men by a tiny handful of custodians can be accomplished only by an all-permeating regimentation of activity that is unvarying from day to day. Long lines of men have to be moved from one part of the institution to another; they must remain in control on the way and the count must be the same when they arrive at the cell block as it was when they left the activity area.

Regimentation becomes essential in such a situation and in this the warden has little choice, although some of the forms of regimentation are vestigial. Generally, the inmates will be more perceptive than the staff in noting that some practices have only historical meaning rather than any current usefulness. Take, for instance, the way that all the little amenities of life are rationed in a typical prison. This is particularly apparent in the dining room, because it is in prison dining rooms that trouble has always been expected. Though most prisons have modified their dining room furniture in recent years, there are still many with the traditional bench-table combinations that seat all prisoners facing the same direction. This was a security measure from the days when convicts were required to eat in complete silence, using hand signals to request more coffee, etc. It reflected the great fear the custodians had of gatherings of all prisoners in one place where a spark of anger could touch off a revolt of the whole population in an instant. The original design of such dining rooms usually provided a balcony on the end wall where an armed guard could sit and watch the silent faces of all the men.

Such a dining arrangement usually meant that convict runners went through the aisles and started the bowls of food down each bench, a setup which gave the first man the chance to get the best and the most. When a plate of bread came down the row the last man always knew — and resented — that several hands, perhaps washed, perhaps unwashed, had fumbled at the stack before it got to him.

With all deliberate slowness these practices are changing, but the dining room still illustrates the problem faced by any warden who wants to make changes. He not only has to overcome the fears of staff who protest that his plan to replace the benches with free-standing tables is a security risk, but he must also get a substantial appropriation out of an uninterested legislature. There is tremendous cost involved in unbolting the benches, filling and smoothing the numerous bolt holes, and buying all new tables and chairs.

Whether prisoners eat while sitting on one-way benches or at four-man tables placed casually around the room, there usually are amenities lacking which the free citizen takes for granted. Salt and pepper shakers were a rarity in prisons until recently. Pepper is still absent from tables in many institutions, for sometime in prison history it was used as a weapon by being blown into the eyes of a guard. But now most wardens who care about the quality of institutional life have recognized that the inmate who wants to attack a guard will find the means one way or another and will not be stopped by the mere absence of a pepper shaker.

Another common courtesy, the provision of paper napkins, was a real prison innovation when started at the Minnesota State Reformatory in 1969. Before then the prisoner was just never supposed to need to wipe his mouth or fingers.

When regimentation is the accustomed means for economical operation and security, it can lead to the avoidance of decision-making, based on the satisfying premise that everyone is being treated alike. This can be a virtue up to a point, but, again, to the inmate it comes through as phony and artificial. An example is the typical prison rule against the wearing of rings. If a prisoner has a ring that is valuable, or one that could be a serious weapon on the leading edge of a fist, it makes sense to pick it up and hold it for him among his other personal effects. But a wedding band is not a weapon and is seldom an object of theft; yet it is often banned along with other rings. Why? Because staff finds it easier to apply the rule broadly instead of having to make distinctions, and the custodians are not usually appreciative of the psychological implications of denying a man this symbolic link with his family.

Regimentation Becomes Monotony

While regimentation is a function of management, boredom becomes a product of regimentation — a more colossal boredom than any the average person has ever experienced.

Nothing is more normal or basic to human nature than the need for occasional variety. Consider the endless ways we seek for change. The typical company cafeteria serves reasonably good food at minimal prices, yet with more or less regular frequency the employees travel out of the neighborhood to eat somewhere "different." We get terribly tired of eating lunch at the same place every day — that is, all of five meals a week.

A convict eats every meal, about twenty a week, at the "company cafeteria," with no option ever to go somewhere else for a change.

We like frequent changes of clothing. Even if the office worker wears the same suit several days in a row, he varies it with different shirts and ties from day to day. The typist will never appear in the office wearing the same dress on two consecutive days. Furthermore, we are accustomed to changing clothes once or twice in the same day.

The convict wears the same uniform every day of his prison life, and sees everyone around him in identical clothes. The heavily oppressive nature of this sameness is apparent in the risks that inmates will take to vary their clothing even a little. Unable to wear different or individual clothing, a man will often try for some individuality by getting special treatment of his clothes by the laundry. Typically the men working in the laundry can make a bit of under-the-counter income by putting starch or extra sharp creases in pants or shirts. Often both the laundryman and his customer may be risking disciplinary action by this deviation from the standard, but any tiny bit of individuality is worth some risks in prison.

Most people enjoy having a job that has variety in it and whether or not the job is interesting we obtain diverse activity from our free-time pursuits. The automobile and the freeway have become all-important, not just to get us to work and back, but because we want to go places, to see new scenes in our spare time.

A convict goes to work every morning at his assigned job which is usually menial and uninteresting. It is only a short distance from his "residence," and he walks to it in company with the same men he has been seeing in the same line for months. He does not have the privilege of varying the routine by taking a different route to work on some wayward impulse. He may be in a prison for months or years and never move from cell to shop except on the identical route every day, with no chance to stroll about other parts of the complex. There may even be lines painted on corridor floors to mark the space within which he must walk. Never is there a vacation to look forward to and if there is ever a break in the routine it is likely to be for unwanted reasons such as illness. At the end of the work day he goes to lift weights or play cards with the same bunch in the same place in the yard. At night he is locked into a cell that is so exactly like perhaps 500 other cells in the same block, stacked three or four tiers high, that if his name and number were not on the door he could identify it only by counting down from the end of the long row. He cannot go away for a weekend trip. In fact, the weekends are especially boring, with the shops shut down, more cell time to put in, more cards, more of the same old faces.

Of course, there may be a movie. While the rest of us can choose our movies and the time we want to go, the convict sees movies that someone else has selected for him and at a time of someone else's choosing. Television? Yes, tuned to a channel that someone else has chosen. Probably anywhere from a dozen to fifty men have to use the same set, and to avoid the inevitable bickering about which program to watch, a committee makes the choice.

Life without Privacy

To the deadly prison characteristics of regimentation and boredom add the resented condition of never having privacy.

Consider all the ways in which the average person protects his privacy. When our country emerged from its frontier state with the frontier's minimal services and comforts, among the niceties it reached for most enthusiastically were the aids to privacy. Where once even unacquainted travelers had to share the same room in a hotel, we hurried as quickly as possible to build hotels with private bath in every room. Private homes with two or three bathrooms became common as fast as our general affluence would permit. For everyone, normal living seems to call for moments of complete privacy, quietness, calm.

The convict ordinarily can achieve complete privacy only illicitly. If a prisoner is out of everyone's sight it becomes a risk situation. He might be engaged in some activity that threatens the security of the institution, so the prison building and its operation are designed to keep each man always in view. For instance, if he were working anywhere in the free world he could go, when necessary, to the men's room and have the brief privacy of an individual booth. But in a typical prison shop the nearby "men's room" is a urinal and row of toilets in a corner of the larger shop room, separated only by a light partition of about shoulder height. This permits uninterrupted supervision by the officer no matter how personal the activity. It is the same when the man is in his cell. The toilet is fully visible to anyone walking by. Defecation is a public affair in a prison.

Closely akin to privacy is the simple blessing of quietness, and a few days spent in prison will give anyone a new appreciation of just how much of a blessing it is to have occasional moments without racket. The prison is a chamber of noise and even late at night sleep may easily be disturbed by a variety of sounds that echo through the cell blocks. The building itself is the worst contributor to the problem. Prisons are built with primary concern for security, durability, and ease of maintenance, so all surfaces are hard and smooth. Floors are concrete or terrazzo; walls and ceilings are hard smooth plaster or masonry. Every surface echoes every sound. Carpets, drapes, ceiling acoustical tile — all the things which serve to deaden noise in any other kind of building are absent in most prisons.

To compound the problem a prison has a great capacity for making noise. The gang locking and unlocking of rows of cell doors is clangorous. Even the opening or closing of just one door during the night makes an echoing racket which affects the sleep of several hundred men. Classrooms or any rooms where counseling, group discussion, or family visiting take place will often have the same bad acoustics, making it difficult and unpleasant to hold conversation.

Although prison staff members are aware of the problem, they still are not likely to appreciate fully its oppressiveness. They live with it only eight hours a day and then can get away to places of their own choosing.

The massive cell block with its endless rows of identical barred rooms has bothered many institution planners, and upon occasion new facilities have been constructed with open dormitories. This appeals to many as being less prisonlike, eliminating the punitive-seeming barred cells. But a fairly usual result is that prisoners, if they have a choice, will take the cell instead of the dormitory. It is not that they like the bars and their incessant clamor of opening and closing. It is, instead, that a cell is individual space, even though it is not privacy as we would like it. That front wall of bars leaves the occupant forever open to view, but it is more private than the open dormitory and so is preferable.

A curious outcome of this quest for privacy is the kind of usefulness that some of the very early prison cell constructions may sometimes have. The original Quaker concept was to give a man a large enough cell to live and work in practically all of his time. Such a cell was completely masonry instead of having one wall of bars. It was found to be untenable to keep a man in such a cell every moment, since human nature needs companionship more than it needs privacy. Later, because of the damaging effect on permanently isolated prisoners and because of increasing prison populations, these cells were crowded with two or three men each, a situation which destroyed any usefulness such construction might have had. Philadelphia's notorious Holmesburg Prison preserves intact these large cells with their tiny doors and arched ceilings; each was intended to be living and working space for one man, but now there are three men in most of them. In the Missouri State Penitentiary, however, an original cell block with the all-masonry enclosed cells is now serving more usefully than it ever did before, this time as an honor block. The cells house one man each, as originally intended, but instead of being used as continuous lockup they are for men who are allowed to move about with extra freedom. The cell doors are not locked. The heavy walls not only give complete visual privacy but also make the cells quiet and cool. It is very much the preferred living situation in that institution with the opportunity it affords for privacy beyond what is ordinarily possible in prison.

The Frustrations of Medical Practice

When one is sick, even more important than privacy is the availability of medical care, and no complaint is more universal and persistent than that about prison medicine. Sometimes it might even be uncertain who complains the most — prisoners or prison admin-istrators. Wardens often find that providing good medical service is one of their most frustrating tasks, and seldom is anyone satisfied with it. In general, prison inmates have a higher incidence of illness than is typical in the outside population. Prisoners come predominantly from among the poor and disadvantaged and this means poorer nutrition as children, more neglect of health, more untended injuries. In the outside world they might be considerably tolerant of their own conditions, but in prison they will show a sudden interest in getting medical attention. There are two factors involved in this, and both are part of the human nature we all share. One is the boredom of prison life. Going to the doctor is something to break the monotony. The other is the prisoner's feeling that since the state has deprived him of his liberty he will get back all he can from it, and this will certainly include treatment for every last ache or pain.

Coupled with these relatively simple factors is the high percentage of persons in prison populations with neurotic anxieties which emerge in psychosomatic complaints that are difficult to diagnose. This kind of problem is especially vexing to a jail administrator who is constantly presented with complaints from prisoners who are new and short term, for he has not had the chance to get to know them as a penitentiary warden knows his longer term prisoners. The jail superintendent, usually without a doctor on his staff, is harried with medical decisions he must make almost daily. The prisoner may be faking or imagining his severe pain, and to call a doctor or send the prisoner to the hospital will present opportunities for escape, will tie up another guard or two for the hospital run, and will put a further drain on the jail budget.

On the other hand, if the pain is real and the condition potentially serious, and if the superintendent guesses wrong on it, the prisoner may die or suffer other serious consequences and then there is public outcry and scandal about a callous jail administration. It becomes particularly ominous in a large city jail where arrested persons are being brought in at all hours of day or night. Particularly during the late night when no nurse or doctor is on duty, an arrestee may arrive in obviously sick condition. If it is only intoxication he can be put in a cell to sleep it off. But usually it is up to an admitting officer with no medical training to decide whether it is only a simple drunk or perhaps a diabetic coma or some other condition that needs immediate attention. One way or another the medical problem becomes a trap in which both prisoners and jailors are caught practically every day, and most unfairly.

Not only is the demand for medical service heavy, but the quality of service offered is inadequate in just about every prison. Furthermore, the conduct of medical service is frequently at odds with other aspects of prison management. The reasons for these problems are found sometimes in low budgets, but are just as likely to be inherent in the modern character of medical practice and its incompatibility with prison management.

A full-time doctor is often nearly impossible to find because doctors would rather practice elsewhere than in prisons. Nurses may be downright afraid to work in a prison hospital. With professional salaries being much higher than correctional salaries, the state usually finds that a full-time doctor would have to be paid more than the warden whom he works for, and approval for this is not easily gained. The usual result is that prison hospitals are often staffed with part-time or on-call doctors only, and sometimes by a superannuated person who has been persuaded to come out of retirement. The experience with the elderly and tired doctor ranges from tolerable to dismal.

Medical treatment today depends heavily upon the use of pills, and doctors who practice in prisons do not expect to have to change their customary methods. The result is that the custodial staff is harried with the need to handle the distribution of hundreds of medications each day. The daily logistics of setting out in hundreds of tiny paper cups the pills required by all the inmates under treatment, of getting the right pill to the right man, might seem no more of a challenge than making the same sort of daily distribution throughout the wards of a large hospital. There is a characteristic of prison life, however, which makes the process more worrisome among the cell blocks. This was pointed up somewhat dramatically by an incident which occurred at the Minnesota State Reformatory for Men.

Following a very minor incident on the reformatory yard one evening, the men returned to the cell blocks in that mood of excitement that tells staff to expect trouble. In one cell block the men ran entirely wild, refused to enter their cells, and proceeded to break their way into adjoining office areas. In one office they came upon a locked metal cabinet which contained most of the institution's drug supply — dozens of bottles of pills. The cabinet door was pried open and the bottles grabbed. All the men who were near took pills by the handful and swallowed them without paying any attention to what labels were on the bottles.

By the time the disturbance could be brought under control in the next hour more than twenty inmates were unconscious. In fact, the ingestion of the pills helped terminate the riot because so many of the leaders had knocked themselves out. As soon as control was gained, other prisoners joined with staff and ambulance teams to work over the comatose men, several of whom would have died without the prompt attention.

The irrational, senseless act of swallowing the pills indiscriminately tells something significant about the quality of prison life and also about the problems of medical service. These men were not suicidal, nor would they have shown any remarkable need for pills had they been outside. But these were men used to freedom, movement, variety, sexual activity; and instead they had suffered months of the boredom, regimentation, and deprivation that is just what prison is all about. Taking pills and having something crazy happen to one's body or mind is a sad substitute for more normal satisfaction, but it is better than no kicks at all.

Prison guards are well aware of the prison drug culture and are often distinctly uneasy with their job of dispensing pills. It is distressing enough to think that someone might get the wrong pill, with serious consequences. The guard has the additional worry in knowing that some inmate will try not to take his pills, saving them to sell to another inmate, or saving them to take a larger number at one time, or that perhaps other potentially dangerous games are being played.

There is one other kind of dilemma confronting the warden in providing medical services. Modern medical practice is dependent upon use of sophisticated equipment so expensive that even hospitals find it difficult to finance many of the major equipment items. The typical large prison has a hospital, but it has a limited patient load to serve and cannot possibly afford the equipment needed for the diagnosis and treatment of many illnesses. Prisoners consequently must be taken to neighboring hospitals for such service and the prison budget not only must pay the high hospital costs, but must also provide the transportation and the twenty-four hour per day guarding. One state penitentiary, located in a rural area, takes its prisoners when necessary to the small hospital in the nearby town and leaves them there unguarded by just securing one ankle to the bed with handcuffs. The key is left at the nurses' duty station for use when the man must be taken to other parts of the building. However, most hospitals — and wardens too — would be horrified at such a practice, and wardens elsewhere glumly accept the fact that hospital care will be extraordinarily costly, and, guarded or not, hospitalized prisoners frequently will manage to escape.

Altogether, the area of medical service gives the warden one of his most persistent sources of frustration, since it seems impossible to make the quantity and quality of service meet the demand. In his own mind the warden may be satisfied that he is doing everything that should reasonably be expected, but there is always the lurking possibility that he may guess wrong on someone's complaint and be faced with a suit for failure to provide needed hospital care.

The "Privilege" of Work

Seldom do judges engage anymore in the formal whimsy of pronouncing sentence with the additional phrase "at hard labor." Apparently they have discovered what a hollow pronouncement it is. If it is truly the court's intent to sentence an offender to hard labor, prison is by no means the place to send him. As with any other generalization, there are exceptions to such a sweeping statement, and these are worth noting first.

It was the expectation of much of the early prison development that the prison should be run without cost to the taxpayers, meaning that the prisoners would do enough productive labor to pay the operating costs. The Minnesota State Reformatory for Men, built about 1890, was located at St. Cloud where there was opportunity to develop an extensive granite quarry. The intent was to have convicts quarry the granite, build their own prison with it, and then pay for the institution's operation with the continued quarrying and sale of granite. The first goal was accomplished. The institution is a massive gray monument with a wall so extensive that it encloses not only the complex of buildings and recreation yards, but also two granite quarries. It is said to be the second longest prison wall in the country. However, by the time the massive construction job was finished, the market for granite was no longer so strong and the institution never achieved its goal of self-support. Similarly the Colorado Penitentiary at Canon City operated a quarry for many years, and the Kansas Penitentiary at Lansing operated a coal mine.

Another Minnesota institution, the prison at Stillwater, managed to operate without legislative appropriation during many of its early years because, as a service to their mostly rural constituents, the legislators had authorized the prison to make farm machinery, rope, and binder twine, and these had a steady, profitable sale.

There were other early examples of self-support, but when staff members demand a forty-hour week and when labor unions and manufacturers' associations oppose prison-made products on the market, the prison cannot hope to pay its own way. The most recent to give up this struggle has been the southern penal farm type of institution. Reputedly, the two prison farms in Arkansas, for instance, never had received any appropriation from the state legislature before 1968. In fact, they actually made a profit which the legislature relied upon every year. This was one state in which a judge actually could sentence a man to hard labor and mean it. But it brought Arkansas no reason for pride. Until recent years the Tucker and Cummins prison farms in Arkansas operated with an incredibly small handful of staff, so the payroll, the big budget item in most prisons, was exceedingly low. But this meant using inmates for most of the operational and even managerial functions. The most notorious aspect of this was the use of armed convict guards. It also was necessary for everyone to work long hours; twelve hours per day was the usual rule for staff and inmates alike. There were no counseling or rehabilitative services to use up the farm profits. Everyone worked in the fields, and productivity was enforced by beatings and other refinements of torture nearly unbelievable in twentieth-century America. The brutal mistreatment of prisoners was unknown to most people outside the prison farms and ignored by those who did know it, but finally it was noted by an indignant federal court and as a result the self-supporting prison is only now disappearing.

Now it is time to find a solution to the contrary, and much more pervasive prison problem — idleness.

Even in the prison that has work enough for all its inmates the eight-hour day is achieved only by staff. The ponderous demands of prison management interfere constantly with the inmates' work schedules. Every day the staff must take a thousand or so men who are assembled in cell blocks and reassemble them in different groupings according to the variety of housekeeping jobs, the shops, and the other details. They must be recounted and marched off by groups to their work. The noon lunch hour must be long enough to permit reassembling them all at the dining room, feeding them, and again rearranging them in new groups for afternoon assignments. A prison considers itself rather efficient if it can maintain a six-hour day for inmates. It also considers itself very fortunate if it has enough work assignments for them all. The tragic situation, found much too often, is the prison which must let perhaps hundreds of its men sit in complete idleness every day because there is no work for them.

As if all the counting, recounting, assembling, and marching were not enough, prison shop foremen have as much or more absenteeism to contend with as any outside shop would have. Individual prisoners are called out to see the doctor, the dentist, the chaplain, the caseworker, the parole board, the classification committee, the disciplinary committee, a visitor. Even when the prisoner is actually on his job it still may not be much of a job. Many prisons have to stretch the available work and do so through extensive featherbedding. To keep prisoners from being entirely idle every work detail may be overloaded. Two or three men are responsible for mopping a patch of floor that properly would justify the efforts of just one of them.

So the system has been caught between the excessive, callous work assignments on the self-supporting prison farm and the soft pretense of work in the underprogrammed walled institution; neither one an experience calculated to help the inmate toward a wholesome respect for the world of work.

Then there is always the issue, growing more intense these days, of whether the prison jobs have training value. Usually they do not, and often we comfort ourselves by thinking that at least they teach good work habits. The honest prison administrator makes no such claim.

It would seem eminently sensible for prison shops to be of those kinds that would train prisoners in trades that would give them useful employment upon release. Undoubtedly every warden in the country agrees with this and fervently wishes to run his prison accordingly. But for all practical purposes it is nearly impossible to accomplish. As one interesting example, the U.S. Penitentiary at Leavenworth, Kansas, has an enormous and modern shoe factory, run on a solid production basis. The several hundred men assigned to it gain excellent training on various machines and could certainly qualify for work in shoe factories upon release. But for most of them the training is wasted. Probably no more than one in a hundred comes from a town where there is a shoe factory.

Another type of problem is offered by some of the other kinds of prison industries. The print shop, for example, should be a useful industry for training since there are print shops everywhere. But the trouble with this particular trade is that printing machinery is constantly being modernized and the competitive outside shops tend to utilize the latest equipment. The prison budget rarely can afford to buy an expensive new machine to replace an old one just because it is no longer popular, so a prisoner's training is valueless when he finds himself entirely unacquainted with the modern machinery in outside shops.

The production shops that are unrelated to outside opportunity are increasingly a source of resentment for prisoners. The black prisoner, already incensed at the lack of occupational opportunity which played its part in his entrance to crime, is incensed all the more when he finds himself in prison working at something that makes money for the state but adds nothing whatever to his marketable skills. In Minnesota the prison twine industry made an excellent income for many decades until it was finally phased out in 1971. Prisoners were sharply aware that practically nowhere else in the United States could they find any work making twine. But as long as they had to keep the twine shop in operation it delayed the day when they would be offered more useful experience. Actually, that institution had an excellent program for training in typewriter and adding machine repair, a skill that is marketable almost anywhere. But, typical of most such programs, it could handle about half a dozen men at a time, while the twine shop employed several hundred.

Plagued by the cost of equipment, by the lack of teaching staff, by the great variety of vocational areas to serve, and by the opposition of unions, the usual warden will probably agree that prison can never be justified only as a place to educate, to train, to teach work habits. Economic factors all seem to work against the prison, and in respect to work programs, an appreciable part of this problem is the immense resistance to the competitive sale of prison-made products. From both labor unions and manufacturers' associations come stiff objections to any prison industry that results in a product for sale. So again the prison administration is caught between two impossible demands. Prisoners need to be trained in work habits and productive labor instead of being kept in idleness. But it has to be honest labor. The old idea of empty, punitive work on the rock pile is as passé as the Dodo and a sure incitement to disturbance. On the other hand, meaningful work — truly instructive work — ends in a product, and that is a political liability.

The dilemma is usually resolved by playing a game which sets up a myth of avoidance of competition. This emerges as the "state use" laws which provide that prison-made goods will not be sold on the open market but will be used only by state government agencies. So furniture made at the state penitentiary is sold only to state hospitals, colleges, or governmental offices. Prison garment factories produce pajamas for patients at state hospitals or uniforms for the highway patrol. So easily we deceive ourselves, for in fact every item sold to a governmental agency means one less item that private industry can sell to government. The private entrepreneur not only has his market cut by the prison production, but he is even prevented from open competition with that product line, since it is typical for state laws to *require* governmental agencies to buy first from the prison.

Nor is the prison product necessarily any more of a bargain. Often the business manager of a state agency finds that he could get the product he wants cheaper and quicker if he could order from a private industry.

The proper direction that prison industry should take will be discussed further in chapter 9, but it should be apparent already that it is, first of all, a most complex issue and that it must be resolved eventually in favor of the inmate and his training, rather than in favor of financial profit to the state. Like all other issues, this too ultimately boils down to a problem of money.

If any major prison is truly going to provide realistic job training, counseling, individual therapy, and even decent, enlightened personal treatment of prisoners, it will need a budget much in excess of what any typical prison receives now. But this is not at all likely to happen. In any legislature today there is constant worry about taxpayers' revolts. Taxpayers are even defeating bond issues intended to improve their own children's schools. At the same time there is a demand for the improvement of highways, hospitals, higher education, garbage removal, housing, police protection, pollution control, and many other services for which there is not enough revenue.

In the public esteem the prisons are low on the list, if indeed they are on the list at all.

CHAPTER 3

The Meaning of Noncommunication

GEORGE BERNARD SHAW, who had more than a passing interest in the prison problem, wrote about some of the people he knew who had stimulated his awareness of the uncivilized character of prisons. "I knew Prince Peter Kropotkin who, after personal experience of the most villainous convict prisons in Siberia and the best model prison in France, said that they were both so bad that the difference was not worth talking about."[1]

If this unhappy observation is valid, it may be partly owing to one of the major characteristics common to all prisons — the deprivation of communication.

The human need to communicate is so well recognized and so often stated that it becomes trite to belabor the point. But this very ordinariness becomes significant when we note that what is so utterly taken for granted in society is conspicuous for its absence in its prisons. The typical prison employee might express some surprise at such an allegation, pointing out that the usual prison has generous enough visiting and correspondence privileges. Once or twice a month a prisoner can receive a visit — closely supervised, of course.

[1] George Bernard Shaw, *The Crime of Imprisonment* (New York: Greenwood Press, 1946), p. 9.

Once or twice a week he can write a letter. So he is allowed to communicate.

But the real communication for which human beings hunger is not just a formal exchange of information at regulated intervals. It is a qualitative condition that is composed only partly of the exchange of information, and more importantly is a sharing of presence, and mood, and feeling. It is a thing of gestures, glances, caresses, and even shared silences. It is this poignant togetherness and nonverbal touching of the spirits that constitute the real quality and need of communication, whether or not any substantive information is exchanged. But for the most part the usual prison policies on communication screen out its more human quality and permit only the exchange of information.

The enormity of this denial is again something that most free people will barely appreciate. For most of us a postage stamp is easily available, and we are seldom more than a five-minute walk from a mailbox. The privacy of our mail we take for granted. Telephones are everywhere, and we can put dimes in the slot and talk to our heart's content. Communication is so easy and such an integral part of our style of living that we rarely think of how vitally we need it or how bereft we would be to lose it.

[It cannot be said that the prisoner is without communication, but it is very limited and so subject to controls that it becomes another source of deep frustration and resentment.]The telephone, for all practical purposes, is simply not available to the prisoner. Usually in a prison there is a way in which a prisoner can make a phone call if there is a family emergency or some other important situation which necessitates it. But this may mean, for instance, that he must get an appointment to see a caseworker, itself no small accomplishment, and then persuade that busy person that he has an unusual and urgent reason for calling someone — altogether a process that easily engenders resentment against being treated so like a child.

Ironically, being denied use of the telephone hits a person just at that time when he is most in need of very active communication. It is important enough to have the comfort of talking with a friend or family member when in trouble. But it may be downright crucial to reach someone who can give concrete help, and to pursue that contact fully. Nowhere can the denial of communication be more traumatic than in the typical jail where unconvicted persons are held. Such a prisoner is terribly reliant on the assistance of an attorney, a bondsman, or a family member who may help to obtain bail or prepare his case. But harried jail officials can allow one phone call, two if they are generous, to the new prisoner, and this is rarely enough.

Here is where a great American source of pride is found to be hollow. The defendant is innocent until proven guilty, we have always proclaimed. A magnificent concept, but a defeated one when we do not permit the prisoner the simple means of communication to obtain the help that he cannot give himself while behind bars. There is little comfort in being innocent if one is, nevertheless, locked up in jail and unable to do anything to prove that innocence. Even if the one phone call reaches and engages a lawyer it still is not sufficient. Lawyers are busy people, and the lawyer will work along on the case at a speed that seems reasonable to him without bothering to give his jailed client frequent reports of his progress. One of the cruelest forms of refined torture is the denial of the telephone to the prisoner who is sitting week after week in jail, wondering if his attorney has forgotten him, unable to get in touch with him in any way to find out what is happening out there among all the lawyers, judges, and others who are playing with his fate.

But this is not to say that the custodians are deliberate in maintaining this additional put-down. There are reasons, not all of them good ones, for denying phone calls by prisoners. One is simply the cost involved in providing enough phones to serve an inmate body of lonely men who would make extremely heavy use of phones if they were freely available. Another concern that the custodians always have is that prisoners would use the phones illicitly, calling friends on the outside to arrange help in escape plans, harassing disliked persons with threatening calls, or just making nuisance calls as a means of relieving boredom. These are not necessarily valid reasons for forbidding phone calls. Escape planning by a determined inmate is not going to be foiled by denying him access to a telephone. Other problems could be controlled by the simple expedient of having a prison staff member place the call and determine first the recipient's willingness to talk with the caller. However, this does get back to the problem of cost and administrative problems. It would take extra staff, equipment, space, and the budget for such to make the calling possible and this effectively prevents this form of communication for the time being. It is one more indicator that decisions by prison management are made in the interests of economy and staff convenience rather than with concern for the normal needs of the inmate.

But to be fair to prison administrators, it should be pointed out that the problem is larger than just a prison problem. Its solution must involve all the other concomitants of the criminal justice system. Consider the sort of problem found in any large urban jail — Philadelphia, for example.

On July 4, 1970, Philadelphia's Holmesburg Prison had a riot which was remarkably vicious and bloody considering the absence of any actual fatalities. Subsequent investigation showed an important causal factor to be the high percentage of inmates being held there as detainees awaiting trial and sentencing. Holmesburg was originally a prison for sentenced offenders, but in recent years the number of men awaiting trial had become so great that about half of the more than a thousand inmates were detainees. There is a standard assumption that an unconvicted prisoner may not be required to work, and the effect often is that little effort is made to provide work for such men even if they would work voluntarily. Holmesburg had little work and much idleness, even though some of its detainees were staying for a year or more.

The riot investigation report noted the nearly unanimous belief of everyone involved "that the prime source of the frustration which fed the violence at Holmesburg Prison is the prolonged, uninformed uncertainty which faces detentioners there. Many prisoners complain and many defense counsel frankly admit that on many occasions lawyers are too slow in making contact with their clients and too casual in keeping their clients informed as to the progress of their cases. Prisoners are often brought to City Hall for trial and returned to prison totally ignorant of the reason they were not tried. Apparently when defense attorneys obtain continuances for tactical or other reasons — or when the prosecutor must ask for a continuance or the court cannot hear the case — they often do not fully explain to their clients why they must spend another month in jail untried."[2]

Though the detainee has his special needs for communication, the sentenced prisoner too is often deeply frustrated and anxious about outside problems. Prisoners as a group tend to have nagging personal problems, frequently of a legal nature. The prisoner's family has trouble, say, with the landlord; sometimes there is a separation action or divorce in process; child custody becomes a problem; and always family support is a worry. If these are not enough to cause a need for communication, there is just the daily loneliness which makes mail so vital. Nevertheless, the prisoner's right to correspond has always been severely limited owing ostensibly to the custodians' fear of what he might write, but also owing to a vague fear of unknown administrative problems if correspondence is not tightly controlled.

To prevent the type of correspondence that might jeopardize institutional security, censorship of mail is one of the most universal prison practices. Censorship in turn has the effect of limiting correspondence since there is never unlimited manpower for reading letters. So, again, in the interest of economy and staff convenience the prisoner must confine his letter writing to an approved list of family members and write no more than a limited number of letters per month. Perhaps the major put-down involved here, though, is the petty rules imposed upon the character of the letters. In some prisons a check-off sheet is used by the censor in rejecting any outgoing letter that he has reason to stop. When sending such a letter back to an inmate, the censor can supply a copy of the list with a check mark by the appropriate reason for refusing to let the letter go out. One such sheet has the following choice of reasons for rejecting a letter.

[2] "Preliminary Report on the July 4, 1970 Riot at Holmesburg Prison," by James D. Crawford, deputy district attorney for law. Unpublished report of investigation conducted jointly by the Philadelphia District Attorney's Office and Police Department. P. 62.

Addressee is not on authorized correspondence list.
Addressee has been removed from your authorized list.
Addressee is a former inmate of this institution.
You have referred to an inmate or former inmate.
You have criticized institution personnel.
You have criticized institution policy.
Your letter contains indecent language.
You have used more than one sheet of stationery.
You have not used regulation stationery.
You have altered regulation stationery.
You have not signed your full name to your letter.
You did not write your number on envelope flap.
You did not write with ink. (Never use pencil or red ink.)
Write on lines only.

The average free person would find it deeply galling to have to comply with such requirements in the course of writing a letter to his mother, for instance, even just one time. The prisoner, denied phone calls, denied daily contact with family, and dependent heavily on letters, must comply with these artificial rules with every letter he writes, perhaps for years.

Lately more generous policies are being adopted in most prisons, dispensing with all censorship of outgoing mail, while incoming mail is opened and inspected only as necessary to remove money or contraband. The growing acceptance by prison administrators of this relaxed practice is in interesting contrast to their previous rigid defense of mail censorship. The real impetus for the change has come from court decisions that insist on the inmate's right to privacy of his correspondence, and as the custodians get used to the imposed change they find their prisons actually operating as well as before. It could cause a thoughtful warden to wonder how many others of his stoutly defended procedures could safely be modified for more human effect.

The Visiting Room

Of course, the best form of communication is the personal visit with family or friends, and here too the prisoner is subjected to restrictions that cause bitter resentment. Under even the most generous policies the prisoner is often tormented by his inability to maintain contact with his family. In many cases the institution, serving an entire state, is far from the homes of its inmates. A federal prisoner may find himself so far from home that his family can never afford to travel the long distance to visit him. Prisons were seldom built with any consideration for the accessibility of public transportation, and many families of prisoners have no automobile. Visiting hours may be very specific and bear no relation to the time of day or week that some families have available for the trip. These are some of the reasons why it is often observed that men who stay in prison for an appreciable amount of time seem to have fewer visits as their sentences wear on, and may eventually be badly neglected.

The major issue regarding visiting is its physical setting. The traditional physical barrier is still in use in many prisons and is, in effect, one more bit of subtle cruelty. Most often it is seen in the large jails where presumably it is not as bad since they were meant for the brief holding of prisoners awaiting trial or serving very short sentences. But this is no longer any comfort since jails are now usually clogged with prisoners who are there for a year or more, even awaiting trial.

The physical barrier sometimes is a heavy screen through which the voice will pass, but not contraband articles. In other arrangements it is a solid glass which permits a better view of the visitor but necessitates use of a telephone. The opportunity to see and talk to a wife, a child, is a precious one, but it leaves a sense of hurt and frustration when it is impossible to embrace, to kiss, or even to touch.

A strong trend has developed toward liberalizing visiting privileges, and in many of the prisons there are now lounge-type visiting rooms in which a man may visit with his family in a natural way. Sometimes the setting includes an outside area with picnic tables, lawn chairs, and play equipment for the children. These changes are a humanizing touch that could have been introduced long ago. But institution administrators did not fully appreciate the forms of dehumanization that have always characterized prisons. Then, too, public support has always been on the side of firm, hard, no-nonsense prison administration, and this means no great concern for the sensitivities of the prisoner, or perhaps a gross misunderstanding of those sensitivities.

The righteous free-will concepts that nurtured the country's beginnings tended to encourage a very somber approach to our dealings with the criminal. The warden of the first state prison in Maine was not at all unique in his feelings, but more gifted with dreadful eloquence than most when he penned, in 1830, his own view of the proper character of a prison.

State prisons should be so constructed that even their aspect might be terrific and appear like what they should be, dark and comfortless abodes of guilt and wretchedness. . . . The convict shall be furnished with a hammock on which he may sleep, a block of wood on which he may sit, and with such coarse, though wholesome food as may be best suited to a person in a situation designed for grief and penitence; and shall be favored with so much light from the firmament as may enable him to read the New Testament, which shall be given him as his sole companion and guide to a better life. There his vices and crimes shall be personified and appear to his frightened imagination as the co-tenants of his dark and dismal cell. They will surround him as so many hideous spectres, and overwhelm him with horror and remorse.

We would like to think that such a view would not gain wide support, even in that day, but Warden Daniel Rose did in fact have the legislative and public support to design, build, and run his prison with literal application of such concepts.

Another reason administrators have not hastened to liberalize correspondence and visiting privileges is that there actually is some risk involved, and a warden must be prepared to assume such risk and to try to persuade his staff to accept the more generous practices — something that is by no means easy. Person-to-person contact in a visiting room is an invitation to smuggling, and in the operation of a very large maximum security prison it becomes seriously important to block every effort to smuggle in any weapon. A gun among the inmate population will sooner or later get used and someone will get hurt, whether or not an escape is accomplished.

In more recent days the growing drug problem has added

another risk to the open visiting arrangement. Presumably the introduction of drugs through the visiting room can be blocked by having the inmate strip completely and submit his clothes for search after his visit. But the intimate quality of the strip search can be highly resented, making it one more example of the indignities that go with prison. And so the warden who has gained a point in permitting a more natural visiting situation loses it again in the necessity to have a prisoner searched in all the private recesses of his body on the way out of the visiting room.

Here again it is a matter of saying that while prisons are in desperate need of improvement, while we can and must do many things to make them less dehumanizing, they, nevertheless, have inherent characteristics which always will partly defeat our efforts. The demands of regimentation, custody, and control become uppermost and every attempt at liberalization increases the risks in respect to orderly, secure operation. As we move along the range from the largest and most secure to the smallest and most open institutions, we find that the closer we get to the latter the closer we are to the feasibility of a flexible operation that permits dignity and individuality — or nearly so.

Perhaps it appears by now that all this is only trivia. There seems nothing profound about the problems of regimentation and boredom or the difficulties of mailing a letter or managing visiting privileges. Somehow the problem of prisons must have grander dimensions than that!

So it is trivia. But that is exactly what is profound about the total issue. It is the commonplace that gets overlooked and neglected. And the usual popular attempt to analyze prison problems is the clearest example of this. It is not necessary to look for a venal warden, or even a merely inept one. It is not necessary to look for sadistic guards, political chicanery from the governor's office, inadequate food, or stingy budgets from an uncaring legislature. By and large these kinds of problems are less than they used to be. When we look for such factors we are missing the real guts of the problem which is that in the best of prisons with the nicest of custodians and the most generous of kitchens, the necessary minutiae of management tend to deny and even insult the basic needs of individuals. It may seem absurdly inconsequential to a harried prison administrator that a prisoner does not like having his mail censored or does not have free access to a telephone. But it is all part of the profound and significant matter of communication between human beings as well as the inner psychological needs of each person. Personality health requirements so basic as these cannot be tampered with except at serious risk. Sooner or later the prisoner must lose his spirit, or he must rebel. And of the two, rebellion is the more healthy in its derivation, if not in its immediate outcome.

CHAPTER 4

The Noncorrectional Institution

WITHOUT BEING aware of it, we are highly ambivalent about rebellious behavior. It was much to be commended in our forebears when they engaged in rebellion against George III. Outright defiance of authority was heroic when Patrick Henry challenged the duly constituted government with a call for armed resistance and declared, "If this be treason make the most of it!" We even applaud rebellion in prison when it is a matter of stalwart American soldiers resisting brainwashing in Communist military prisons, or plotting and carrying out escapes from such.

But the plotting of escapes, the resistance to brainwashing (i.e., treatment, counseling, etc.), or the engaging in any insubordinate behavior in a domestic prison is regarded in an opposite manner; it is condemned as proof of villainy. In this context tragedy lies in the fact that so many men adapt to even the worst of prisons, meekly conform, and quietly survive at the expense of subjecting their spirits and losing their pride.

Of course, this is a dangerous generalization to make, for the psychology of human adaptation is extremely complex and admittedly there are times when a man's quietly conforming survival in a repressive prison may be the result of his own superior intellectual control. A disciplined mind which is able to maintain perspective and to find internal means of preserving its integrity will survive without the necessity of overt rebellion. Though more prisoners with this quality of self-discipline are being admitted to our prisons as a result of increasing social protest efforts, many more of our prisoners still are not blessed with intellectual maturity and self-discipline equal to that challenge. Prisons are the repositories of the poor and inadequate, people who take direct action and who, as a part of their limited perspective, reach for satisfactions of the moment even though their impulsive actions will be self-destructive in longer range terms.

So, given a prisoner with this type of action pattern, an act of insubordination in a prison, self-defeating though it may be, will often have to be analyzed as a clumsy but hardy effort to maintain self-respect.

It seems a bit ludicrous to compare Patrick Henry's challenge to King George with the insubordinate act of a prisoner who gives an equally rebellious response to a correctional officer's order. The two situations are poles apart in the public regard; but, like it or not, in terms of basic human psychology they are the same.

This is not to argue that defiance and rebellion in prison should be rewarded, or even tolerated. While the prison exists it must be managed safely and this means that overt rebellion has to be put down. It also means, however, that we are basically and deeply wrong when we set up a "correctional" institution that simply cannot be operated unless it reverses normal human psychology, punishing the prisoner for acts of insistent individualism and rewarding him for something we call "good behavior" but which in the prison context may in fact be a tragic surrender of self-pride.

In order to run a prison at all and to control its massive population, we have had no choice but to reconstitute certain standard virtues. Where regimentation is so essential individuality must be discouraged, and so it becomes a vice rather than a virtue. And the emasculated man who is scorned in the competitive world for his spineless compliance may be the model prisoner who is rewarded with early parole.

Having to Live with the Guards

One common daily element of the struggle to retain self-pride is the interaction between prisoner and guard. It must be said, and emphatically so, that there are guards in every prison who have a genuine concern for prisoners and a desire to treat them with all fairness. This is to give the immense credit that is due to those individual officers everywhere who have kept prisons relatively stable and have been of very true help to many individual prisoners.[1] But this is not enough. More commonly the prisoners' contact with officers is more of the put-down, even though the officer does not intend it to be so.

After respects are duly paid to the exceptional officers, it must be said that these are far too much a matter of luck, for prisons almost invariably hire officers at the high-school education level and ordinarily obtain relatively unskilled persons who are not in demand elsewhere. Here and there efforts are being made to recruit young men who will come to this work as a career, but so far this is unusual. More often they gravitate to it as they do to any local industry. Many of our prisons are in small towns where the prison is the major industry and employment there is a family matter. When this is true it is a condition usually pointed to with pride as evidence of integrity and stability. However, stability can also be stagnation. When son follows father into the local prison service, he may well be carrying with him the accumulated and entrenched attitudes of the past generation and so the new face on the staff does not really represent the freshness that a new generation should bring.[2]

[1] The potential opportunity that the prison staff has but seldom realizes is suggested by Gaddis and Long's *Killer* where the remarkable story is told of Carl Panzram, a fiercely dedicated criminal who was executed after a career that included twenty-one murders and apparently hundreds of barely lesser crimes. Panzram seemed completely depraved in his hatred of the entire human race and he pursued this course with dreadful consistency through his whole life. There was just one person he ever had any sympathetic feeling for, and because of that one man we have the data which were supplied by Panzram himself and are the major substance of the book. Though Panzram was especially bitter about prisons, the one man he became friends with in his entire life was a guard in the District of Columbia jail.

[2] An example of a prison that dominates a town is the Montana State Penitentiary, located in the very small town of Deer Lodge. The varsity team at the local high school is named the "Wardens," while the junior varsity is the "Deputy Wardens."

In choosing sites for prisons it has been common political practice to place them in rural areas represented by the most persuasive legislators, usually with the argument that jobs are needed there. But this does not suggest that prisons can pay high salaries. Corrections officers are usually paid less than industrial workers in the same area, and officers typically work on second jobs. At the time of the violent riot a few years ago in the Jackson, Michigan, prison half the guards there were moonlighting. Offering low salaries, the prisons often must recruit industrial shop workers who have been laid off or construction workers who are tired of a job that is too seasonal or too much outdoors, or that requires frequent moves to inconvenient job sites. Such a man is endowed with good Horatio Alger virtues and a supposition that since he himself has worked hard and honestly for what he has the usual prisoner could have done the same if it weren't for laziness. Such a person is a credit and an asset to his community, but not to a prison. He has little understanding of the very different life experiences of the usual prisoner, and he assumes that what the prisoner needs is a bit of what his own father occasionally gave him in the woodshed. He may not be at all mean, but he lacks sensitivity to the special feelings of the imprisoned person, and this has the effect sometimes of being more offensive than sheer malice might be.

The inherently brutal or sadistic guard is so rare that this hardly need be considered a problem, but this is very little comfort, since the problem we do have is almost as provocative and so much more subtle that it is more difficult to isolate and correct. Consider this anecdote from about sixty years ago that involves the Minnesota State Prison which at that time was chronically infested with bedbugs. "An afflicted prisoner one day stepped up to the deputy warden, respectfully gave the customary military salute, and, with a solemn face that would do credit to a judge about to impose the death penalty, remarked: 'Say deputy, I have a complaint to make.' 'All right, proceed,' said the deputy. 'Well,' continued the prisoner, 'there are about five hundred inmates who pass my cell every day going to and from their work and each man throws a bedbug into my cell. This d—— foolishness has to be stopped or there will be something doing,' and the man looked as though he meant business. Telling of the incident afterward, the deputy said that the story was so absurd he could scarcely refrain from laughing."[3] The sad aspect of this story is that it was written by a long-time employee of that prison who included it in a small book which was intended to tell about what a fine institution he worked in. He saw no reason to think that the high quality of his prison was the least bit denied by the staff's unsympathetic laughter at the inmate who presumed to protest a little thing like bedbugs.

These days we keep our institutions free of bedbugs, but the same insensitivity to prisoners' feelings is still all too common. Sometimes there emerge those racial or ethnic slurs that seem innocuous to the guard who utters them but which are deeply galling to the inmate. It would seem a minor thing indeed if a guard, when speaking to an Indian inmate whose name he doesn't remember, were to address him as "Chief" or "Sitting Bull." There may not be the slightest rancor with it, and the guard may be in a friendly, even jocular mood. He may be incredulous if told that his remark is racist, for he himself perhaps has been addressed in less complimentary terms without getting upset.

It is a common phenomenon that even the person who daily works in a prison is not perceptive to the meaning of prison for its inmates. The man who lives in the free world, who is secure in his knowledge that he is a competent person with an established place in his social group, is a man who can shrug off insults, and even with some amusement. But the inmate is in a position which is humiliating enough even if he is otherwise well treated. Additional slights are far more abrasive to him, especially since defense and retaliation are not permitted. In other words, the inmate is denied the masculine, self-assertive recourse of striking back, either verbally or otherwise, or even the milder action of demanding an apology. All he can do is swallow his pride and inwardly seethe. If he happens to have poor self-control he may lose his temper, strike the guard, and spend days

[3] William Casper Heilbron, *Convict Life at the Minnesota State Prison, Stillwater, Minnesota* (St. Paul, Minn.: privately published by the author, 1909), p. 54.

in solitary confinement. Suppose, however, he does only what he would be able to do as a free man on the outside, that is, demand an apology. If he does this in any traditional prison he is in for trouble, for this is a challenge to the authority of the guard and unless the guard is an unusually secure person he will not tolerate such loss of face; so the inmate gets reported for insubordination. The custodians instinctively feel that to permit any instance of challenge from any inmate would be to invite general loss of order.

This went so far in many prisons to include a rule against "silent swearing." Though this offense may no longer be officially recognized in any prisons, many prisoners have gotten disciplinary reports for allowing their facial expressions to show their feelings of the moment.

Notwithstanding the friction that often develops between guards and inmates, critics tend to ascribe to the guards too much cleverness in their manner of subjecting the prisoners. For instance, they are accused of deliberately provoking dissension between whites and blacks in order to keep inmates from uniting against the staff. Other such allegations contend that the custodial staff follows a systematic plan for breaking individual spirit and group unity as a designed means to control the inmate population. Admittedly, custodial staff actions often are just as mean in effect as if they were diabolically calculated. But for the critics to ascribe to the guards a conscious, sophisticated kind of psychological warfare against their prisoners is to overestimate the custodians badly. To the prisoner it may seem pointless to argue that his mistreatment derives from the guards' obtuseness and naïveté rather than from their callous cleverness. The effect of it is just as hurtful either way. However, if we are going to work to correct the problem we should not be misled by its nature, but must know with some clarity just what it is that we are attacking.

An episode occurred in one state prison that helps to illustrate fairly typical staff behavior in aggravating situations. It involved a prisoner, Mr. H———, who was quite intelligent although he had had a persistent criminal record for twenty years or more. He was deeply hostile toward all authoritative persons and with his very quick mind, coupled with his contempt for just about everyone, he was superbly skillful at annoying people. In prison he was so frequently brawling with other inmates and being insubordinate to staff that much of his time was spent in "the hole."

During one prolonged period in segregation Mr. H——— was unusually obnoxious toward the guards. When his meal was brought to him he would occasionally knock the tray from the guard's hands, sending the food into the officer's face and all over his uniform. Another trick was to save up a cupful of urine, then call a guard to his cell and throw it on him.

Such acts were accompanied by and interspersed with obscene taunts especially galling to his guards. One day Mr. H——— was particularly loud, particularly persistent, particularly infuriating, and the guards, in addition to their own bitter annoyance, had cause to be concerned about the other segregation prisoners. They have to listen to the furor too and it raises the tension level disturbingly. Presumably for this reason, but more because he had had all he could take, the guard took action to quiet Mr. H———. He shot a capsule of tear gas into the cell.

The immediate result was indeed that the prisoner quieted down. But the success of the action was only illusory. Viewed from any angle, it was a mistake. It was a simple lashing back at an intolerable irritation, an essentially primitive response by a guard who was acting as an all too normal human being.

Hardly had the tear gas cleared before Mr. H——— got out paper and pencil and prepared a writ which was quickly sent to the nearest court, alleging cruel and unusual punishment, etc. Mr. H——— was clever at that sort of thing and his competently formulated writ received prompt attention. He did not get what he most wanted — release — but he did get the court to order that no prisoner should be gassed if he is safely confined alone in a single cell. Gas should be used only when it is necessary to control unconfined persons and protect lives and property — not just to quiet a verbally obnoxious prisoner who is not otherwise a threat. The court's decision was a reasonable one, but the custodial staff felt it as a rebuke and repudiation.

Even a fairly simple examination of the episode shows that the guard's instinctive action was self-defeating. If he had been well trained he would have understood his own reaction better. He would have known that by gassing the inmate he was only satisfying his own need to win, to prove that he had the power to command silence and enforce the command. But he also would have realized that by winning in an immediate way through superior force he was actually establishing his own defeat, for the effect was to place the inmate in control of the situation by giving him a basis for court action against the guard and the institution.

If the custodians were as clever as the critics contend, they would not engage in endless variations on this same type of mistake, or at least they would learn by their mistakes, which they all too seldom do.

Some of the Louisiana State Penitentiary history illustrates the ancient problem of the unqualified, untrained guard with too much power and also the problem that confronts any administrator who tries to change something so committed to the status quo as is a traditional prison staff. The Louisiana institution operated for many decades as a farm whose profit to the state was far more important than its corrective effect on inmates. In 1941 the then governor Jones learned of the frequent and severe floggings being given inmates at the penitentiary and he ordered that no more floggings were to be given under any conditions whatever. Three years later the new governor Davis discovered that floggings had never ceased and he too ordered an end to the practice. After another two years an outside study team evaluating the institution found that floggings still had never stopped. It was apparent that the wardens had never passed on the executive orders to the officers under them, though even if they had it was supposed that it would not have made much difference.[4]

It was quite clear that even then conditions did not improve substantially, for in 1951 the Louisiana newspapers were headlining the discovery that thirty-seven convicts had cut their heel tendons in protest against "overwork, brutality, control by political appointees, and lack of recreation, rehabilitation, decent housing, and edible

[4] Mark T. Carleton, *Politics and Punishment* (Baton Rouge: Louisiana State University Press, 1971), p. 144.

food."[5] It takes more than an executive order to change the practices that a prison guard sees as right and essential to the job he is doing; he has to be shown convincingly an alternate method that will serve as well.

The deliberate mutilation of something so essential as the Achilles' tendon obviously occurs only under the stress of extreme conditions, and Louisiana is not the only state that has faced this kind of protest. Nor has this happened only in the past. Nearly twenty years after the Louisiana rash of mutilations the Kansas Penitentiary was contending with its own series of heel slashings.

Perhaps the most persistent problem with guards from the prisoners' viewpoint is that guards, being human beings, are easily capable of error, but, wrong or not, they still are always right in any encounters with inmates. Every day guards must give orders, rebukes, disciplinary reports, etc., and often with no staff witnesses present. Sometimes the officer may be wrong or, equally bad, the inmate may just believe he is wrong. Nevertheless, the inmate has no chance to prove his innocence whenever he allegedly makes an error. He considers it hopeless to protest since the disciplinary committee is not going to accept his version of the episode over that of the guard's. Furthermore, if the inmate did manage to win his point and get the guard's action reversed, he still has not won a victory that will give him any comfort. Usually the inmate will not even try to fight against disciplinary action because he knows that a guard who has been made to lose face has plenty of resources for retaliation.

A pair of lawyers who have worked with many prisoners express the idea still more strongly. "The central evil is the unreviewed administrative discretion granted to the poorly trained personnel who deal directly with prisoners. . . . Prison becomes a closed society in which the cruelest inhumanities exist unopposed. . . . Finally, any prisoner who dares to protest the system, either orally or in writing, may be subject to further punishment. . . . Such practices produce feelings of abject passivity or murderous rebellion in those whom the prisons purport to reform."[6]

[5] *Ibid.*, p. 136.
[6] Philip J. Hirschkop and Michael A. Millemann, as quoted in the *Minneapolis Star*, September 17, 1971.

The major impediment to any effort to ameliorate this general problem is that inmates and guards have such widely different perceptions of what is going on, and each has so little capacity to grasp the viewpoint of the other. Generally the custodians are comfortably satisfied that they are good fellows doing the best they can to be fair under trying conditions and that if any inmate is dissatisfied with the process it only means that he does not fully realize what is best for him, or he, like the other prisoners, is always trying to beat the system anyway.

At the same time, the inmates see the custodians as part of a phony system which publicly talks about rehabilitation but then plays silly games, dispensing major and summary punishments for violation of the most petty and meaningless rules imaginable. The prisoners note that correctional administrators make speeches and write articles for journals espousing the good American virtues in their institutional programs, but prison life as the inmates actually feel it still requires them to forget the old American virtues of honesty and industry, adopting instead the constant cagey pretense that is demanded if they are to avoid harsher interactions with the custodians and fellow inmates.

But usually the guards' imperceptive handling of prison discipline is the result neither of stupidity nor of ill will (notwithstanding the occasional painful exceptions, of course). Nor are the cynical view and the manipulative survival technique of the prisoner just other aspects of his criminality. It is an inherent and tragic characteristic of the prison world that these two groups of men can live together in elbow-rubbing proximity day after day for years and still have opposite perceptions of their experience with each other. And whatever its implications for disciplinary practices, it speaks profoundly about the near futility of offering "treatment" in this context.

A rather startling experiment, pointing up this whole problem, was tried in a 1971 summer school class at Stanford University. The instructor, Dr. Philip G. Zimbardo, hired about two dozen normal, well-adjusted young men to participate in the experiment which was intended to simulate prison conditions and run for two weeks. Half of the men were picked as guards by flipping a coin. The remaining men were designated prisoners. Before the end of one week the "guards" had become insensitive and punitive beyond any expectations. Dr. Zimbardo reported, "There were dramatic changes in virtually every aspect of their behavior, thinking and feeling. In less than a week, the experience of imprisonment undid (temporarily) a lifetime of learning; human values were suspended, self-concepts were challenged, and the ugliest, most base, pathological side of human nature surfaced. We were horrified because we saw some boys (guards) treat other boys as if they were despicable animals, taking pleasure in cruelty, while other boys (prisoners) became servile, dehumanized robots who thought only of escape, of their own individual survival, and of their mounting hatred of the guards. . . . About a third of the guards became tyrannical in their arbitrary use of power, in enjoying their control over other people. They were corrupted by the power of their roles and became quite inventive in their techniques of breaking the spirit of the prisoners and making them feel they were worthless. Some of the guards merely did their jobs as 'tough but fair' correctional officers. Several were 'good guards' from the prisoners' point of view, since they did them small favors and were friendly. However, no 'good guard' or any other one ever interfered with a command by any of the 'bad guards'; they never intervened on the side of the prisoners, they never told the others to ease off because it was only an experiment, and they never even came to me as Prison Superintendent or Experimenter in charge to complain."[7]

The old truism that "power corrupts" clearly asserted itself with Dr. Zimbardo's students, and rather than denying the value of education, his experiment emphasizes the need for an additional sensitizing kind of training for the guards. But it also reinforces the view that prison tends ultimately to defeat our most humane intentions. Such an assertion may seem unfair to the many prison administrators who are both eager and sincere in their desire to run their institutions with fairness. However, the better ones among

[7] From an unpublished report by Dr. Zimbardo.

them will admit that while their efforts will reduce mistreatment, it will never be eliminated, for the problem is too deeply inherent in the character of the prison.

Living with Other Prisoners

Usually prisoners are allowed to write sealed letters to the warden, commissioner, or governor. One Minnesota prisoner wrote to the commissioner to protest the mail distribution system, which was only the typical practice of having an inmate runner deliver mail to the cells after it had been opened and read. "I resent," he wrote, "having my mail delivered by a convicted felon."

A somewhat startling assertion to anyone who has not felt what it is like to live among other prisoners. Here was a man who was a convicted felon himself. Why should he be disturbed about another such person delivering his mail? But what seems almost amusing here to an outsider is terribly serious to the prisoner. In fact, for many men the worst thing about being in prison is having to live with other prisoners.

Each man sees his own felonious conduct as unique, and he sees himself as not such a bad guy. On the other hand, he well knows that his unwilling companions are unstable and untrustworthy people. He may feel no more sense of rapport with other offenders or have no more trust in them than the average man in the street does. Admittedly, if his only fear were that the mail runner might read his mail, this would be a minor cause for worry. But the fear is far more serious than that. Prison is a barely controlled jungle where the aggressive and strong will exploit the weak, and the weak are dreadfully aware of it.

What first of all gives this fear reality is the grossly distorted society in prison. Consider first the more normal large social groupings that all of us experience: a college student body, a church congregation, the fellow employees at the office or industrial plant. We join such groups voluntarily, we feel some degree of loyalty to the organization and its purposes, we see some personal advantage in its progress and prosperity, we share a sense of common interest, trust, and rapport with other members of the group. Our contentment with belonging to any such group is enhanced by the knowledge that we are free to separate from it whenever we wish, for whatever reasons that may appeal to us.

By contrast, the prisoner is in a large, social group which reverses all these conditions. He did not select the organization (prison) or the companions it imposes on him. He has no sense of rapport with them and certainly no sense of trust in them. He feels not the slightest loyalty to the aims of the organization that presides over his care and custody. Furthermore, despite our brave talk about time off for "good behavior" and the parole board's opportunity to reward such with early release, the motivating factors for each prisoner are still mostly negative.

Rewards in prison are shadowy, insubstantial, and terribly uncertain. A prison invariably lists for its inmates many rules and the various punishments that accompany any infraction of them. But it would be rare to find a traditional prison with a list of behaviors for which stipulated rewards will be given. Punishment is always an immediate thing, but the rewards — favored job assignments, reduced custody level, furloughs, and perhaps assignment to work-release or other "outside" status — are achieved only after an uncertain period of time and are based upon criteria that remain somewhat esoteric as far as the inmate can determine.

If an inmate is to be punished by being sent to "the hole" for several days, there always seems to be space available there immediately. But if he thinks he has earned assignment to some favored status or job, there may be protracted delays while he must wait for a space available or for mysterious red tape to untangle. Prison officials may privately admit that a prisoner has ostensibly met all the behavioral requirements for the reward of some job reassignment or new status, but they may have some reservations about his stability, his type of original offense, or many other possible factors, and so be reluctant to move. The prisoner, not being told the reasons for delay, is aware only that rewards are elusive and apparently given on some whimsical basis with much evidence of favoritism.

An apparent change in this condition is found in some of the new behavior modification programs in which specific rewards are posted for specific kinds of meretorious conduct. This is a healthy new sign of treatment orientation in prisons, but if it is not handled very wisely indeed it can perpetuate in a new form an old prison problem. If the good conduct specified is only outward behavior (making one's bed every morning) and not evaluated critically, it permits the same old cynical simulation, or faking, of improvement by inmates who know how to play these games without any real inner change. In fact, simulation of improvement is probably the most effective defense against the necessity of accomplishing real improvement.

Not only are punishments more swift and certain than rewards in the usual prison, but by and large the punishments from fellow inmates may be much more to be feared than those from the staff. Grudges develop easily in the close, confined, and tense life of the prison, and are likely to be settled with direct and fearful action. Any prisoner who has reason to fear any other prisoner knows well enough how easy it is to make a knife in prison — and how easy it is to use it. Life becomes a continuing terror for him since he has no place to hide, no route of escape from another prisoner who can take his time and wait for the most opportune moment. A typical large prison cell block may hold up to 500 cells and during the evening shift there may be only two guards in the immediate area. The 500 inmates watch television, play cards, or just move about the cell house in a variety of personal activities. It is impossible for guards to observe all the action and it is far more common than the public thinks that somewhere in this group a man will suddenly slump with a knife in his back.[8] Perhaps every man in the area knows who wielded the knife, and why. But when questioned they know nothing. They have to go on living in that prison and they realize how little their own lives would be worth if they talked. No warden would boast that he can truly protect an informer except by transfer to another prison, and not even that will always suffice.

Certainly many men go to prison and manage to maintain

[8] To use the California experience as an example which is probably not untypical, there were 134 inmates killed by other inmates during the period 1960–71, a rate of one per month.

neutral relationships with other prisoners, remaining unthreatened throughout. Just as certainly, many men are natural victims in this setting which encourages others to be natural predators. The predator arises from the same circumstances that foster exploiters anywhere else. Where there is a shortage of a desired commodity, scalpers, smugglers, black marketeers, or others will provide the commodity for a price. In prison there are endemic commodity shortages that are among the saddest that men endure. Here where food, shelter, and clothing are fundamentally sufficient, men are lacking the psychological needs of love, companionship, excitement, variety, and release of tension and anger.

It is possible for a well-financed and well-programmed prison to keep the resultant problems at a minimum, but more frequently our old cell blocks, our inadequate programs, and our minimal staff permit the development of an inmate jungle that may be vicious beyond the imagining of the average person. One of the better documented examples of this tells of the experience of the three Philadelphia prisons which in their design tended to encourage disorder and defeat control and which for years were victims of budgetary neglect. Despite the administrators' repeated efforts to impress the public with the need for prison reform, a shocking condition of sexual depravity gradually developed among the inmates until it finally came to court attention. Consider the account of James Banon, an eighteen-year-old inmate. This is one of many such episodes detailed in the investigation report that was submitted to the court.

Banon stated that he has been in Holmesburg since March, 1968 and that about a week and a half ago, on Thursday he was in "I" block, his cell was number 926. On this date in the morning after breakfast Jack Wendt called him into his cell, he went into Wendt's cell, Dick Richie was in there also. Further that he had owed Wendt 4 cartons of cigarettes. Wendt said to him that he would have to give the cigarettes back right now or he would have to give them something else. He (Banon) then started to walk out of the cell and Wendt pushed him down, Wendt picked up the window pole, Richie picked up a bench and stood blocking the door. Richie told him that if he goes to the guard they are going to get him anyway, there were other men outside the cell.

Further that he walked out of the cell, they were all around him and walked to cell 971 and they pushed him inside. He went over and sat on the toilet seat (clothed). Blip Jaeger came into the cell, they made him lay down on the floor and Blip pulled his (Banon's) pants down and made him lay face down, Blip pushed his (Banon's) legs apart and Blip put his penis into his (Banon's) rectum, he was on him until he discharged, when he got through, Banon saw that he was bleeding from the rectum. Then Blip, Wendt, Richie, and Malvern told him that if he went to the guard their boys would get him to "D" block and he was scared then to tell the guard. Further that he did cry out when Blip did this to him but the guard wouldn't be able to hear him because the block is long.

Banon went on to say that the next day after chow (breakfast) Jack Wendt, Malvern, Smith, and Livingston got him in cell 972, they told him that everything is cool now as long as he doesn't tell. Further that he had never been in jail before and he was too scared to tell anybody. Then four of them did it to him, they put their penises into his rectum. Blip did not bother him that time. That after they did this he was bleeding and got sick.

That night Randall (Tim Randall) came into his cell and changed with his partner. Randall told him that he would have to do it. When the guard came to check the cells, Randall turned over so he wouldn't be recognized. After the guard counted and left Randall got on top of him, put his penis into his (Banon's) rectum and discharged. [9]

This exhaustive investigation, covering a period of two years up to July 1968, documented 156 such sexual assaults and concluded with the carefully considered and conservative estimate that probably the actual number of assaults in that period totaled 2000.

Two of Philadelphia's prisons were built with the concepts of a century ago, with very large cells that had solid walls on all sides and a small door. It was intended that each cell would hold only one man, but with the later inevitable overcrowding the cells had to house two and often three men each. In addition, there was no way to lock the

[9] Report on Sexual Assaults in the Philadelphia Prison System and Sheriff's Vans, by Alan J. Davis, chief assistant district attorney and special master. An undated and unpublished report of an investigation conducted jointly by the Philadelphia District Attorney's Office and Police Department. P. 19.

cell doors from any central point, and the cells were on either side of very long corridors. A guard would have to take the long walk down the corridor to lock and unlock each cell individually.

Because the institutions' work program was negligible, most prisoners stayed in and around the cell block much of the day, and with the limited staff there was too much for the guards to do without having to walk up and down corridors locking and unlocking doors. Consequently, doors stayed unlocked most of the time and what went on in any one cell was unobservable to the guard at the end of the corridor. With three men assigned to each cell, the guard could not be expected to distinguish between a legitimate and an illegitimate group in each cell every time. The combination of idleness and constant opportunity for uncontrolled privacy led to gang rapes as a daily occurrence. The investigation report observed that "virtually every slightly built young man committed by the courts is sexually approached within hours after his admission to prison. Many young men are overwhelmed and repeatedly raped by gangs of inmate aggressors. Only the tougher and more hardened young inmates — and those few so obviously frail that they are immediately locked up for their own protection — escape penetration of their bodies. After a young man has been successfully assaulted, he is marked as a sexual victim for the duration of his confinement, and this mark follows him from institution to institution until he returns to the community, embittered, degraded, and filled with hatred."[10]

In addition to citing the defects of the buildings and the staff and program shortages as causes of the sexual assaults, the report also provides a perceptive comment about the psychology of the aggressor. "Finally, most of the aggressors appear to be members of a sub-culture that have found closed to them most non-sexual avenues of proving their masculinity. Job success, raising a family and achieving the social respect of other men have been largely beyond reach. Only sexual prowess stands between them and a feeling of emasculation. When the fact of imprisonment and the emptiness of prison life knock out from under them whatever other props to their

[10] *Ibid.*, p. 3.

masculinity may have existed, they become almost totally dependent for self-esteem on an assertion of sexual potency and dominance."[11]

In any prison there is the continuing daily tragedy that if the prison staff is not strong enough to protect the threatened prisoner, he will inevitably be a victim. The proof of this not only is seen in the occasional rapings, beatings, and murders that occur in any prison, but it emerges still more sharply any time there is momentary loss of control. A typical example was the Kansas Penitentiary riot in 1970, when prisoners took over a cell block and held control of it for several days, barricading it against the guards while they destroyed all vulnerable equipment in it. When the officials regained control, it was found that many of the prisoners had taken no part in the riot, had stayed most of the time in cells in small groups. Three or four inmates would barricade themselves in a cell, securing the door by whatever means they could improvise, and sleeping in shifts so that someone was always awake for their mutual protection.

In this kind of situation some prisoners have no wish to join the rebellion and they fear the instability of those who may turn against them. Others are men who are already marked; they live in awareness that they will be the victims of someone's vengeance any time that loss of staff control provides opportunity for the attacker. In a planned disturbance inmates may become victims of inmates within minutes.

In the usual prison there is a handful of "treatment" staff: caseworkers, trade instructors, teachers, perhaps a psychologist and a part-time psychiatrist. We calm our consciences these days by grafting these helping services onto the massive old prison.

And this book is not written to say that we should not do so.

But it is monumentally difficult to administer a healing touch in a matrix so fraught with fear and constant invitation to distrust.

[11] *Ibid.*, p. 38.

CHAPTER 5

The Defeat of Management

IN THE WEEKS following the Attica rebellion, criticism of that institution and its parent department was lavishly bestowed from all sides. One editorial comment made the point that the New York State commissioner of corrections had conceded that most of the inmates' demands were justified and the problems they reflected should have been corrected before. So the rhetorical question was asked, "Since [the commissioner] has been in office eight months, why then were they not corrected before the riot?"[1]

It would be very nice indeed to believe this to be a reasonable question. Instead, it is painfully naïve because any prison system is exceedingly complex and not that easily manageable. The New York correctional system, particularly, presents an overwhelming administrative challenge. The new commissioner who was supposed to have the department's problems solved in his first eight months in office was confronted by a domain that included over 7650 employees and more than 15,000 prisoners in twenty-one different facilities. In eight months he could hardly have learned fully what his problems were. Furthermore, even a new warden cannot expect so quickly to make new and lasting changes in his one institution. Often there is

[1] Tom Murton, guest editorial, *Penal Digest International*, September 1971.

61

the illusion of rapid change as a new administrator comes in and makes some specific moves that are reported by a press that is closely watching him. But these sudden changes are likely to be deceiving because they do not become real until they are accepted, at least without any overt opposition, by both staff and inmates. Until then change is superficial and most uncertain.

In one state prison, for instance, and a typical one in this regard, there is a deputy warden for custody and under him a captain who is in charge of all custodial staff. The two of them together represent about sixty-five years of experience at that institution. Furthermore, the deputy warden, with his nearly forty-five years of service, followed his father who spent his entire working career at the same prison. But what of the warden? And what of the commissioner? In the last twenty years that institution has had six different wardens, and the commissioners have changed with similar frequency. The point is — in that kind of situation the governor can appoint a new commissioner and a new warden, perhaps both of them real fine fellows; but offsetting the authority of the warden's position is the deputy warden's "authority of knowledge." He knows every nook and cranny of the institution. He knows every staff member and the history of every rule or problem or practice. Furthermore, the custodial staff is going to take its cue more from the deputy warden than from the warden. "Wardens come and go," they will say with a philosophical shrug when some new proposal or policy is initiated from the front office. If the deputy warden clearly supports the new proposal, maybe it will be all right. But he is the one they have to live with year after year and if he gives even the most subtle sign of unenthusiastic reaction to the latest directive this may be enough to make it ineffective.

Of course it will sometimes happen that a staff is ready to welcome and follow a new warden, perhaps because of their relief at being rid of the previous one, or perhaps because the new man has unusual skill and charisma. Much will depend too on the size of the institution. The larger the staff and the inmate population the harder it will be to change. In this country, we have about twenty prisons that house more than 2000 inmates each, and over sixty others with

1000 or more each. Their sheer size alone offers monumental resistance to change which is abetted by another prison characteristic — a military style of staff structure.

Usually in the chain of command the correctional officer is responsible to a sergeant who is responsible to a lieutenant, and so on up. This tends to support a one-way system of communication. Orders are sent down from the top and feedback from below is not encouraged.

Private business and industry are discovering today that systematically involving rank and file staff in the management process is both commonsensical and practical. This may take the form of giving staff at all levels the opportunity to hold meetings for the purpose of setting goals for operational units, planning for greater efficiency, and finding ways to enhance individual responsibility. These are tested techniques that augment productivity, raise staff morale, and reduce staff turnover. The application of such techniques, increasingly common in industry, is needed in the typical prison more acutely than in the usual business setting, but such an effort is rarely seen in prison management.

In many respects the operation of prisons is perhaps half a century or more behind the operation of industry where well-paid executives are selected strictly for their competence and expected to run their companies with the most progressive methods. A product line that is not making a profit is quickly reappraised and either redesigned or dropped. A company president is hired or fired depending on his ability to get results.

Even though this quality of leadership is now becoming more common in top correctional positions, we have yet to overcome the heritage of a century of unconcern about professional prison management. When state governments were young and populations were small, the typical state had no correctional "system," but only an institution, usually a single prison which had to take the whole range of prison types. The warden was then the only corrections administrator in the state. He was usually appointed by and responsible directly to the governor, and he did not have to possess a standard body of knowledge to qualify for the job. Under such conditions it was inevitable that the position should be used for political patronage, and so the early history of prisons — with a few stellar exceptions — was a history of mediocre administration by men who brought no specialized skill to their jobs, often were no more than mildly interested in the work, and always were ready to move casually to something else if the state government changed hands at the next election.

There were some nineteenth-century pioneers who spoke out and administered with intelligent dedication, but part of the reason for their outstanding leadership was the wasteland of mediocrity around them. Even though we have made progress away from that condition, we still are powerfully influenced by the residual effects of that history. There still is no general expectation that wardens or commissioners must be trained either in correctional matters or in public administration. There still are many top administrative jobs filled as political patronage. Fortunately governors are tending now to select creditable professionals for such positions, but no matter how professional and competent the patronage appointee may be, he ordinarily will be replaced by the next governor, with consequent disruption of continuity.

In recent years an occasional commissioner-level appointment has been made of a man from the business world who brings excellent business and administrative ability to the position, but no corrections experience. If such an individual also has a broad perspective and an appreciation of human problems, this kind of selection is good, since it introduces a fresh approach that the otherwise inbred correctional field badly needs. This still is rare, however, and even the most enlightened new administrator finds himself confronted with a monumental organizational inertia that works against efforts to change.

Throughout prison history a persistent negative factor in prison management has been the simple fact that correctional administrators are not in a profit-or-loss situation and have never been required to defend their operations on a cost-effectiveness basis. Admittedly, they do have this kind of concern in respect to the operation of prison industries, and in some states they even have had to be primarily concerned with making a profit. But this has related only to industrial productivity or to the physical maintenance and operation of the facility, not to the process of correcting offenders. In fact, where there has been heavy emphasis upon prison farming or industry profits, there has usually been a consequent reduction of concern for the rehabilitation of the inmates.

The development of any professional management approach has also been delayed since prisons actually could be run without management skill at the top because of the massive physical controls that could substitute for management finesse. For instance, only a few years ago a western prison, following the election of a new governor, got a new warden who, like all his predecessors, was a patronage appointee. He was a rancher who had never seen the inside of so much as a county jail, and any qualifications he had for running a prison were conspicuously absent. He did a lamentable job until another governor and another warden relieved him. Nevertheless, the prison did function and survive even under his leadership. The quality of life inside was degenerate and devoid of any positive influence for good, but all this was held inside by the wall, the guards, the guns; and the satisfied public was not discomfited by the internal conditions. Increasingly sophisticated inmate populations and increasingly inquisitive courts are changing this condition, but as long as the public has not cared, it has been easily possible for the wall to make up for management deficiencies and to screen the inside conditions from public view and concern.

So there have been many factors which have worked against the use of good management principles in prison, but today more than ever the techniques of involving rank and file staff in management decisions are vitally needed. As long as the man at the bottom does not have easy, reciprocal communication with the man at the top, he is likely to resist directives that attempt to change the way prisoners are dealt with. He might be capable of accepting and carrying out a new process with good spirit under certain conditions, but those conditions are seldom accomplished in traditional prison management. If the officer is going to follow a new policy with enthusiasm, he must take some part in the discussions that led to its formulation. He must know what concerns are in the mind of the administrator regarding it. He must have the opportunity to register his doubts and worries, to counter suggestions, and to feel that his views received consideration. Altogether, some new idea in the conduct of the prison will have its best chance of succeeding not only if the officer helped with its formulation, but if it also gives him opportunity for recognition and added responsibility.

This approach seems obvious enough, but when a new warden or commissioner confronts an entrenched institution with 500 or more staff members, and there is no budget to support the process of utilizing the staff systematically in management planning, the inevitable result is that directives are issued at the top and are received grudgingly through the rank and file.

Attica was not the only riot which revealed the lack of staff understanding of administrative planning. The same theme crops up following many such disturbances. The *San Francisco Chronicle* of August 30, 1971, tells of the "Bitter Quentin Guards" following the tragic shoot-out there. A letter of resignation from one of them is quoted: "I am not in accord with the trend toward return of so-called 'normal conditions' at this institution. In order to maintain complete control of the inmate population in a manner which will assure the safety of all correctional officers employed here, there would have to be a sweeping change of administration policies, which, due to many Supreme Court decisions and softened policies by the California Department of Corrections relating to inmate rights, would be an impossibility." Then the Rahway, New Jersey, prison had a riot some weeks after Attica and, once again, a guard was interviewed and quoted (*New York Times*, November 26, 1971) as blaming the riot on "lax prison practices."

This issue of permissiveness involves the whole complex question of just how far we should go in letting inmates share in the operation of the prison. Even those guards who decry administrative softness are themselves part of an informal system of sharing control with prisoners, although it is such an intangible and everyday sort of process that the guard can easily forget the reality of it and persuade himself that the custodial staff is really in total control. But no matter how unobtrusive the process, there is no real doubt that the inmate body does have its share in the control. It is only a question of degree. As already mentioned here, the custodians are vastly outnumbered. Inmates are out of their cells during the day, working in shops and offices throughout a vast complex where the opportunities for mischief are enormous. Inmates carry out duties in the kitchen where there are knives and cleavers. Mechanically skilled inmates are employed in shops where metal-working machinery offers daily opportunity to fashion weapons. Ingenious inmates have also found ways to brew liquor, print counterfeit securities or documents, and enjoy an astonishing variety of surreptitious enterprises. But the prison is utterly dependent upon the willingness of all prisoners to leave their daytime activities and return at night to their cells for lockup. It is equally dependent upon their willingness to keep their activities reasonably and delicately balanced between licit and illicit behavior.

With constant awareness of this fragile truce between themselves and the prisoners, the custodians have always been grateful that prisoners generally are loners and do not ordinarily engage in concerted group action. But this prison characteristic finally is changing, and an increasingly common feature of prison life which is going to effect great change, for good or ill, is the appearance of prisoner organizations. Such an advent can be deeply unsettling to any prison administrator who has always relied on the complete absence of inmate cohesiveness to permit him to control his institution with a handful of staff. The new growth of prisoner organizations has the potential either to disrupt profoundly prison management and control or to improve greatly the whole operation. But whatever the outcome, and whatever the view of prison administrators, prison populations will definitely be turning more and more toward organized efforts. Some prison administrators will support and encourage certain organizational trends; others will oppose them, but will not be able to prevent this development forever. Fortunately they can do much to determine whether the prisoner organization will be a disruptive force or a positive one. It is a challenge that calls for the most sophisticated kind of skill, and is another administrative demand which makes clear that we can no longer afford the politically appointed warden.

The California prisons seem to have experienced more growth of prisoner organizations than have other states. These are organized around such concerns as special problems (Alcoholics Anonymous), self-improvement (Toastmasters), religious interests (Holy Name Society), recreational pastimes (Slot Car Club), and ethnic or racial culture.

It seems useful here to consider the nature of one specific group as an example of some of the administrative and program concerns that it engenders. In San Quentin several hundred black prisoners belong to an organization called Self-Advancement through Education (SATE) which was started by inmates a few years ago. It is a dynamically active group with a schedule of weekly meetings and such bureaucratic characteristics as a steering committee, special purpose subcommittees, regularly elected officers, etc. Its main function is to foster the educational advancement of black inmates.

This organization was by no means conceived of or encouraged by the prison administration. The inmates who originally started it certainly gained no favor by their action. But the administration, after uneasily watching the development for awhile, gradually learned to adapt to it and to help it mature and become a positive influence.

The SATE members are active and aggressive in their advisory service to the prison's academic program, meeting frequently with the teaching staff to discuss curriculum changes that will make the academic offerings more relevant and practical. They will often act to represent the interests of some individual inmate whom they see as needing a specific sort of vocational help.

Perhaps the most healthy element in the organizational life of SATE is that its own members have assumed teaching responsibilities. On their own initiative they worked out a tutorial system for individuals which goes on each evening in the cell blocks. It was also their idea to ask the teaching staff to help them screen and select from among the inmate membership those men who would be competent to tutor other men. Those being tutored may or may not be students in the academic program, but all are persons who want some help in their educational efforts.

Typically, a prison administrator will wonder how soon an organization like this might be taken over by militants who will subvert the group and make it a weapon against the administration.

It can happen. Whether or not it does happen depends upon the skill with which the staff handles the matter. At one point the SATE organization had officers who were clearly attempting to shape the group to their own rebellious purposes. This situation is extremely unsettling to staff, for they find in their midst a sizable number of unstable prisoners listening to incendiary and abusive criticism of staff and administrators. The staff's usual and natural reaction is a protective one, to discontinue the group or to order the trouble-makers excluded from it. The problem with this course is that it tends to reinforce and justify in the inmates' minds the accusations already made by their leaders, and so will polarize the group feeling against the administration even more — exactly what the warden wants to avoid. Instead, the San Quentin staff made no overt move to oppose the militant challenge, but reduced their active cooperation with the group in a mood of watchful caution. This prevented fueling the controversy, and the majority of the inmate group, recognizing in the staff back-off a potential loss of the group's effectiveness, managed to promote a new election and a resultant change of officers.

When an inmate group weathers a crisis like this, the strength and usefulness of the group may be greater than before, and everyone gains. The SATE organization, which had functioned altogether for blacks, eventually produced a spin-off in the form of an inmate-conducted program to help drug addicts, and they were able to accept the staff suggestion that this particular effort, because of the acute need, should cut across racial and ethnic group lines. And so the organization flourishes because it has a mission to perform which accords with the goals of both staff and inmates and because the administration is willing to take the risk of tolerating a prisoner organization.

There is in all prisons some type of accommodation between staff and inmates as they tacitly adapt to each other's leverage in the interests of a tenuous peace. It means in effect that prisoners agree that if they are not pressed too hard on certain matters they will in turn give sufficient cooperation to permit the ponderous institution to operate. The fact of this accommodation is absolute and unavoidable. The only question is just where the balance comes to rest between inmate control and staff control. This will vary greatly from one institution to another, subject to countless factors which, singly, may seem unrelated or unimportant, but which in combination become decisive. At the risk of too simple a generalization, it probably is safe to say that if the balance of control between inmates and staff goes too far in either direction there is grave potential danger.

Sometimes this balance is seriously impaired because of a gross lack of administrative skill, but other times because of such factors as severe budgetary limitations which frustrate the warden's proper control measures. A remarkable example of the latter was a situation which developed in the North Carolina Penitentiary over a long period of time and which culminated in a severe riot in April 1968.

The problem started as a result of certain basic conditions such as an outmoded, century-old physical plant, double occupancy of single cells, low staff-to-inmate ratio, and no wages for inmates. All prisons, whether or not they pay wages to inmates, provide canteens or commissaries where inmates can purchase personal items — tobacco, shaving supplies, toothpaste, greeting cards, etc. The institutional store, in fact, is an absolute necessity, even though it is often a source of irritation too. If no wages are paid, inmates usually get money for shopping from home through the mail or from the sale of handcraft items. Another possibility for some inmates in some prisons is the participation in medical experiments or the sale of blood plasma. Finally there remains the illicit procedure of free enterprise within the inmate population; selling goods, favors, or protection directly to other inmates for the tobacco and other goods or services desired.

In the North Carolina institution handcrafts, especially leatherwork, had become the big enterprise, and although it was a legitimate, sanctioned activity, certain conditions led to its being subverted to illicit uses by the inmate power structure. The first problem was that a high percentage of the inmates, lacking wages, wished to engage in the profitable craft work, but their living conditions put definite restrictions on the amount of such work that could be allowed. With two or more men to a cell, it is impossible to do leatherwork there. So it could be done only in a common room assigned for the purpose, and the only space available was not nearly sufficient to accommodate everyone who wanted to engage in this type of work. The front office kept a waiting list and tried to assign the applicants to the craft work in impartial order. But this was defeated by the inmate power structure.

The most obvious outlet for the sale of inmate craft items is the display counter that is found in virtually every prison lobby in the country. However, the North Carolina convicts had developed a sales channel that was vastly more useful. A certain few convicts, during outside interludes between sentences, had established connections with wholesalers who would take large quantities of craft objects and distribute them through gift and souvenir shops over a wide area. This sales outlet was entirely controlled by the convict bosses. Large packing boxes were regularly sent by mail to the outside distributor, and no items went into those boxes except from convicts who had made their deal with the power group. The deal might be a substantial cut of the take, sexual favors, or anything else attractive as barter. If no tribute were paid it did little good to get on the front office list. One could still do leatherwork, but the lobby display counter would be his only outlet and that was hardly worth the effort. The official list of leather crafters was in the front office, but the only meaningful list was in the heads of certain convict leaders, and most inmates made no attempt to get on the official list unless they were willing to pay the price to be listed where it would count.

It was a process that exploited the work and drained the resources of most of the inmates; it weakened the control of the custodians, and it put vicious and extensive power into the hands of a few convict bosses. In its genesis some years earlier it was undoubtedly a seemingly innocuous small accommodation between staff and inmates, and a reasonable one in view of the state's failure to pay any wages. However, with its gradual growth and ruthless exploitation, Dr. Jekyll had become Mr. Hyde, and when finally it became abundantly clear that the administration would have to reassert its control the time had passed when this could be done without a serious challenge from inmates who would not casually give up their power.

When the administration began the steps to retake control, including plans for a system of wages, the inmate bosses made it frankly and openly clear that they would fight any such take-over. When the custodians persisted in their plan, the convict bosses proceeded to flex their muscles. First there was a fire in the license tag shop, big enough to be a sharp warning, but not so much to be uncontrollable. When that did not stop the administration, a fire occurred in the sign plant, and it was burned out thoroughly. After that the word was passed that the print shop would be next.

At that point the administrators moved quickly and locked up in a separate wing all the known convict leaders. Although this stopped the progression of fires, the convict leadership was assumed by less organized and more impulsive men who were just as insubordinate but who lacked the skill to keep the rebellion under control. The result was a general riot that erupted in the yard at noon one day and ended with the death of six inmates.

There has long been an attitude among prison inmates typified by the saying "You do your time and let me do mine." Prison society is a distrustful society, and every prisoner tends to avoid getting involved in another's schemes unless it might primarily serve his own purposes. The rebellion in the North Carolina Penitentiary involved some concerted group activity, but the participants were not acting out of loyalty to any group except as it served their own individual purposes first. There is an important distinction here.

As long as prisoners have remained loners and as long as they have participated in group activities only to serve their several individual ends, it has been possible to operate a prison with relatively few staff. Yet the custodians in every prison are constantly aware that they are vastly outnumbered, and they know that the prisoners could take over whenever they acted in favor of the goals of the group. Though it seems unlikely that this sort of thing would happen, there are increasing signs that it is a distinct possibility. In September 1971, after long and intricate planning, 111 prisoners left a federal prison in Montevideo, Uruguay, through a tunnel that emerged through the living room floor of a house across the street from the prison. Every prison administrator would recognize the remarkable character of an operation that could be kept so secret through all the time and effort required to do such extensive tunneling. In any ordinary prison the custodians would pick up clues which would lead them to the activity fairly soon. What made the difference in Montevideo was the intense cohesiveness of the prisoner group that planned the escape. They were members of an underground revolutionary organization, the Tupamaros, and as such they had the discipline to work together with common purpose and secrecy.

Of course, this episode occurred abroad, and we are likely to respond with the usual "It can't happen here." However, every year the chances are getting better that it can. Political and social consciousness is a new fact of prison life that has profoundly changed many American prisons. Not only have some prisoners developed a disciplined sense of political mission, but they have also found that they have effective friends on the outside. With this combination prisoners are able to be articulate and to challenge prison management beyond anything that the administrators have previously known or prepared for.

One of the deeply unsettling aspects of prison management today is the fact that prison guards keenly sense these trends and are chronically jittery. They are confronted with prisoners quite unlike those of only a few years ago, prisoners who bristle with a sophisticated militance that challenges the guards' authority in exceedingly worrisome ways. In former days the guard could "demand respect" and get it because he was backed up by a rough, star chamber disciplinary procedure which, the inmate knew, could overreact to any disrespectful behavior and hand out the severest punishment without allowing any appeal. It did not matter to the guard, if he ever considered it, that the respect he demanded and apparently got under that system was only sheer façade and potentially dangerous because of the boiling feelings it hid. For most guards the outward show of respect was enough, but now when suddenly they are expected to deal with revealed feelings they usually have had no training to prepare them for handling that situation, or for handling their *own* feelings, which may be the more agonizing part of the problem.

At the same time it seems to the guard that his bosses, instead of tightening the controls on unruly prisoners, are giving in to them, being too permissive, and letting the inmates get away with grossly threatening and disrespectful behavior. Added to their worries is the growing interest of courts in supporting the rights of prisoners, causing many guards to be hesitant about bringing disciplinary action against prisoners.

One result is that prison guards are far more unionized than they were only a few years before, and through their unions they are fighting back uncertainly but loudly — uncertainly because they are not sure themselves what solutions they seek. Mostly the demands are for some type of direct action that will meet very immediate problems as they see them. They may call for the funding of more positions for guards, salary improvements on the basis of "combat pay," better riot equipment, discontinuance of troublesome special programs for inmates, reduction of outsiders coming into prisons, better insurance and retirement programs for staff, provision of capital punishment for the crime of killing a prison guard.

Generally the demands of worried guards reflect a different philosophy from that óf the administrators and this gap in understanding is a serious impediment to good management. The warden cannot run his prison without some degree of loyalty from his beleaguered staff, and yet with his minimal staff and budget he often finds it literally impossible to set up the kind of communication with them that would promote a mutual philosophy. It is so much easier for the daily operation to widen the gap and deepen the fear than to help unite the levels of custodians. The rank and file staff deal with the short-fused situation at the guard-to-inmate level every day and they know much more about the inmates' potential for rebellion than they know about the warden's plans for eventually easing the problem.

The kind of thing they fear was sharply demonstrated in an episode which lasted only a few minutes, but which had a jarring impact upon the Federal Penitentiary in Lewisburg, Pennsylvania. The trouble started without warning during the supper hour on February 1, 1970. In one of the dining rooms a fight began between a Muslim and a man who had previously dropped out of the Muslim organization. As officers took the aggressor out of the dining room the other inmate, sensing the further wrath of the Muslims, slipped out and hurried back to his cell. Meanwhile, the minister of the Muslims, after learning what had just happened, gave a hand signal and all the Muslims in the room rose and followed him out to find the former Muslim who had been in the fight. It was not a rabble that rushed out of the dining room. It was a disciplined group of nineteen men marching in a military manner. They went to the cell block where their quarry lived and most of them remained in the main doorway while some went looking along the tiers. When a lieutenant came and told them to break it up and return to where they belonged, the group suddenly turned its anger on the staff. The lieutenant was knocked down and kicked as were other guards who were nearby or who came to help. Altogether eight officers were attacked by the inmate group which continued to act in an almost military fashion, systematically kicking the officers so severely that several had concussions and other serious injuries, one remaining unconscious for a month.

After the attack, a matter of five minutes or less, the nineteen inmates marched back to the central control area and remained there, still under the control of the Muslim minister. When the staff then proceeded to lock them up in segregation, they were followed by perhaps 300 or more other inmates until the Muslim minister turned and ordered all of them to return to their cells — which they did. It was a situation in which the staff could be very grateful for the ability of the inmate leader to quiet the population, but it was also an unsettling demonstration that the minister, if he had chosen, could have signaled for more violence instead.

At that hour there were just thirty-five guards (eight of them incapacitated by the attack) on duty — and 1350 inmates.

The walls, the bars, the sally ports, and all the impressive clanging hardware are deceptive in their promise of security. Walls are not the absolute barrier that the public supposes them to be: they serve only to slow down a would-be escapee and make him a better target for the armed guard. And this works only because throughout all the years of prison history prisoners have never had the inclination or skill to join forces in a common aggressive effort that could easily overwhelm their custodians. But that condition is changing, and when the already emerging prisoner organizations become cohesive through heated dedication to a common goal, the prison as we know it will be inoperable.

CHAPTER 6

There Are Also Women

WITH ALL the criticism heaped upon correctional institutions, there is relatively little directed specifically at women's prisons. This may be misleading, for it does not so much suggest less reason to criticize women's prisons as it reflects the more forgotten and neglected condition of them.

Generally, correctional institutions for women suffer from being quieter and so much smaller than the men's institutions that they are pushed aside by legislative and public concern about the more ominous problems of the men's prisons. In comparison with institutions for men that commonly house from 1000 to 3000 or more inmates, there are only nine women's institutions in the United States that regularly hold more than 200 inmates. Twenty-one are under seventy-five in population, and there are five states that usually have no more than ten adult women prisoners at a time.

The small size of these institutions makes them extra costly, even without any rich programming, and so it is typical that a women's reformatory operates at an appreciably higher cost per capita than any other correctional institution. In order to reduce the expense, the women's facility is sometimes located on the same grounds with, or even inside the men's prison, and is run by a matron or superintendent responsible to the prison warden. Especially when the women's unit holds only twenty-five to fifty inmates, it is not surprising that it tends to be a forgotten backwater of corrections, characterized by sterile programs and even more boredom than that suffered in men's prisons.

Before a female offender's case gets to court there seems to be more generosity in screening her out of the system. Women's offenses often are committed in company with males, and a prosecuting attorney will likely be content if he can get a conviction for the male partner; he then may drop the case against the woman or settle for a lesser penalty.

The small number of female offenders is also partly explained by the obvious fact that women are less aggressive than men in any overt criminal sense, and this in turn means that it is not necessary to build so much control into the physical plant of a women's institution. So women prisoners are confronted by less of the massive masonry and hardware, though sometimes the psychology of custody is more repressive in its application by women custodians than it is by men. It might well be hoped that the female custodians would show a bit more sensitivity and compassion than their male counterparts, but such does not seem to be the case. This is evident in the heavily traditional, repressive programs typical of women's prisons and also in the practices around that special concern of the women — their children.

A Place for Children

Years ago the Federal Reformatory for Women at Alderson, West Virginia, followed the practice of allowing inmates to keep their babies, often until they were nearly of school age. There were many of these children at the reformatory, living in the rooms with their mothers and getting much attention also from the other women in the same cottages. To appreciate this situation it should be realized that the physical plant at Alderson bears no resemblance to a conventional prison. The buildings are of much more attractive architecture and are situated on a campus where lawns and trees are far more apparent than any custodial features.

Alderson's practice of permitting babies to remain with their mothers has long been stopped, and corrections workers have a general sense of incredulity that such a policy could ever have been followed. There is a general reaction against the idea of letting a child have the stigma of the prison upon him at that early age. But alternative practices that are followed somehow fail to prove that anyone is using a better approach.

The typical procedure in most women's prisons is to have the pregnant inmate receive her medical care, including confinement, at a hospital in the nearby community, and to arrange ahead of time for the baby to be moved promptly back to the mother's home area. The mother's parents or other relatives may take the child, or, lacking such a resource, the public welfare agency may be given temporary custody.

One institution maintains its own nursery and keeps the new baby there for two weeks to a month before sending it back to its mother's home community. Meanwhile, the mother, whatever her feelings about her child, is allowed to see it no more than once a week, even though it is right there on the same grounds with her. To explain this remarkable procedure, the staff admit that this is partly administrative convenience (there is no nursery in the women's residence buildings and no place for a mother to stay in the building where the nursery is), but they also comment that the mothers show indifference toward their children anyway.

The truth may just possibly be that the mothers, knowing in advance the institution's practice of separating mother and child, handle their hurt by a deliberate shell of indifference, and the staff, long accustomed to the situation, have grown insensitive to the mothers' real feelings. This is by no means subject to proof, but prisons do have this effect upon their employees, and this practice is too frequently complained of by female prisoners to be easily dismissed. Male prisoners too have the emotional problem of being separated from their children, but the male at least can take some comfort from the fact that the children are with their mother and being cared for. The female prisoner obviously has more reason for anguish in the separation.

A sociologist studying the inmate culture at the Alderson institution observed, "A particularly frustrating aspect of imprisonment for the female inmate is that she is not in a position to control the course of events in the outside world; children may be neglected, for example; husbands may become unfaithful or may obtain a divorce; a loved one may die. To dwell persistently on events in the outside world is to run the risk of doing 'hard time.' . . . Therefore, the prisoner must learn — and here her sister prisoners are helpful — to suspend deep emotional involvement in outside events. She develops an immunity to emotional shock to events both within and without the prison gate for the term of her sentence."[1]

Administrators who recognize the unhappy truth of that observation have been concerned about finding better ways to reduce the damage to any prisoner who is cut off from normal family relationships, especially that between mother and child. A compromise philosophy now followed by the Federal Bureau of Prisons permits the pregnant inmate to deliver her baby in a community hospital and then to have a several-day furlough home to get the child settled with her family before she returns to the prison. This is a more sensitive way of handling the situation than is found in most state institutions for women, but it must be hoped that a still better procedure will some day be found. We probably will discover that stigma is not nearly so much a threat to a baby as is the deprivation of maternal care.

The instinctive reaction against raising a baby in prison is a sentimental rather than practical one. The deleterious effect of stigma is mainly related to the impact it has on the self-esteem of the person who is the subject of such a mark. For an infant, rejection by (separation from) his mother is a far more damaging "stigma" than his having to live on the grounds of some correctional facility during the first two years of his life. If he has the uninterrupted care and love of his mother, he has the best chance of growing up emotionally normal and unhandicapped by the physical setting which he will never remember anyway. Depending upon the state, the average length of

[1] Rose Giallombardo, *Society of Women: A Study of a Women's Prison* (New York: John Wiley, 1966), p. 94.

time actually served by a female prisoner usually is between two and three years, even in felony cases. This means that if a baby remained with his mother it would be a rare instance for him to be in prison for as much as four years. Indeed, if the mother were to remain longer than that, some alternative plan should of course be arranged for the child before he has to start to school.

Nevertheless, what about this idea of raising a child in a prison, without the company of other children and with the constant association of prisoners?

Admittedly, most women's prisons, as they are today, are not particularly suited for raising children. Nurseries and playgrounds are not available, and there are no larger-sized rooms to accommodate properly both mother and child. Some of the smaller institutions of fifty or less inmates might find it impossible to adapt to the presence of infants.

But women's prisons will increasingly be developing auxiliary facilities similar to some of the halfway houses, and this may present a solution for mother and child. The day should come — will come — when an institution large enough to have several mothers of infants at a time will have a separate cottage on the grounds or a house elsewhere in which the mothers can live with their babies. A woman with a baby is likely to be only the slightest custody risk, especially if she can stay in an open setting among other mothers and have the opportunity to get to outside activities regularly. It is easy and quite practical to picture a prison annex that would permit some of the mothers to have work-release status and be employed on the outside while other residents help to take care of the children. In the earlier Alderson experience it was felt that not only didn't the children suffer from association with the prisoners, but the various women about them gave them a most helpful, loving kind of attention.

In a separate annex the mothers would have an important common concern and the whole subject area of child care would be a compelling focus of the therapeutic process. Our present approach leads the mother to suppress her maternal feelings in the face of enforced separation from her baby. It may be healthier — certainly more normal — for both the prisoner-mother and her baby if our procedures could instead keep them together and give the mother support, encouragement, and practical counseling in the task and role of motherhood.

Of course this raises the issue of whether the prisoner-mother's other children should stay with their mother in prison. Should the prison allow the mother to have with her any children who were born and living with her before her admission?

The most reasonable answer is to decide this on a practical basis according to each individual case, though this is not the answer that appeals to most wardens. The custodians would usually prefer to avoid individual case decisions by having blanket policies that apply rigidly to everyone and so require no troublesome distinctions. But if it is sensible for a mother to keep with her a baby born during her incarceration it is hardly less acceptable for her to have with her a toddler born the year before. A child who is of school age and sensitive to the implications of the prison setting is quite another matter. It should not be difficult for a wise prison administrator to review the individual family factors, to balance these with institutional housing problems, and to decide upon a rational arrangement for each individual case.

Actually, for most of our female prisoners constructive alternatives could be developed that would make the prison unnecessary, but while the prisons persist we could at least adopt a flexible, reasonable, and humane position regarding the life of mother and child together.

The Therapy of Service

To provide more meaningful work than many women's institutions have to offer and to introduce a valuable treatment technique, a service project can be especially useful. A refreshing example is a program started in Minnesota in 1972, permitting inmates of the Correctional Institution for Women to work as teacher's aides at another institution, a state training school for delinquent boys and girls.

The selected prisoners are processed as they would be for work release and are granted a status known as limited parole. They live on the site of the training school and are given the same pay and assignments as other teacher's aides; in addition to their half day of teaching duties, they work the rest of the time as cottage counselors.

The selection process requires care, of course, although it is appearing possible to assign such work to a wide range of persons. Perhaps surprising is the unimportance of education as a qualification. Women who have accepted homosexuality as a regular style of life are excluded, as are women who regularly resort to assaultiveness. There is little else that categorically excludes anyone from consideration.

The women are under certain restrictions when they first go to this assignment, but these apply only to their time off the job when they must remain on the campus. They live in rooms of their own in one of the institution cottages. After a short period of demonstrating good adjustment to the situation, the women are allowed to go into town in the evenings with permission. Although the experience with the program is very new, it so far is proving to be very useful as a service to the educational program; the women assigned to it are enthusiastic, and there has been no problem in their relationships to their students.

Minnesota also experimented earlier with a child care program that was actually set up on the grounds of the women's institution. For several years it maintained a nursery for retarded children. The institution, in cooperation with the State Welfare Department, adapted one of its cottages to the care of young, severely retarded girls who were wards of the state. Under highly qualified direction a dozen or so prisoners worked regularly to provide the intensive, demanding kind of care that these children required. The issue of stigma never seemed to emerge. The parents of the children were unconcerned about the prison setting and were mainly interested in whether their children received good care. Their general reaction to the program was quite positive. The prisoners who worked with the children, when appropriately selected in the first place, became very devoted to their charges and found the work to be much more meaningful and satisfying than most prison jobs.

Although the program was never formally evaluated, it seemed in its several years of operation to be a most worthwhile venture for everyone involved. It was discontinued in 1969 for necessary administrative and economic reasons which had no relevance to the question of its suitability in the prison setting. The entire experience with it supported the view that the children were not harmed, but helped, and that the opportunity for the prisoner women to function as mothers made life in prison a bit more normal and therefore more helpful to them too.

In this day of liberated womanhood all of this may sound like a hopelessly old-fashioned, sexist view of "a woman's place is in the home." Not so. The woman prisoner should have her own choice. If she decidedly does not want to have her child around her, then she will be happier and have a better chance to adjust successfully if the baby is placed elsewhere. The baby also will be better served if put in a surrogate home where he is wanted than in the care of an indifferent mother. What is argued here is that just as the mother should have the clear right to give up her baby she also should have the clear right to keep it with her. If she has a yearning to have her baby and is going home on parole to be reunited with it after a year or two, she should not have to deaden her maternal sensibilities now in order to survive in the interim, and the baby should not have to have his close and vital maternal care interrupted.

The Barren Life

Without children, without husbands, without neighborhood friends and activities, the women's prison probably more than equals the men's prison in boredom. Perhaps there is some lingering notion that women are more content with quiet activities, or none at all, than men would be. Or perhaps the usual women's institution, being much smaller than the men's, has less flexibility in staff assignments so that not as much activity can be allowed on weekends when staff is light. For whatever reason, it seems evident that the women lead a dull life in most institutions, while in a men's prison at least there may be a Sunday afternoon ball game on the yard. In one women's prison the inmates note with resentment that on Sundays they remain locked in their rooms until 10 A.M.; then they are locked in again from

12:30 to 4:30, and finally locked for the night at 8 p.m. For any normal person Sunday is perhaps the day of greatest freedom. A summertime Sunday brings about fifteen hours of sunshine for outdoor activities, but for these women Sunday means having only six hours in which they can move anywhere outside their own individual rooms. During most of those six hours they still may not go beyond their own cottage, and at no time on Sunday may they play cards or do any washing or ironing.

The administrative explanation is that staff is in short supply on weekends. But where any administrator wants to do so, she can find ways to improve this situation, especially in a women's institution where custody is generally less of a problem than it is with men.

A visit to a typical women's prison is likely to suggest to the observer that boredom and lack of normal mixed-sex activity or contacts have such visible effects as obesity, sloppy grooming habits, and general reduction of self-esteem. This kind of thing tends to compound itself, for a budget-short administrator will too easily assume that substantial expenditures for women's clothing are not warranted in an institution where the women show little interest in their attire anyway. Certainly another factor is that administrators of women's institutions tend to be conservative themselves, or subject to scrutiny by conservative legislators, and they cling quite stubbornly to the notion that their charges should not be dressed seductively. Curiously, it seems to be all right for the women to be dowdy and even downright untidy — but never provocative.

A revealing glimpse of the problem is shown in the report of a student who voluntarily lived briefly as a prisoner and saw something of how the nondescript clothing, regimentation, and boredom are interwoven components of the low self-esteem that institutional life fosters. The observations were made only a few years ago at a reformatory for young women operated then by the District of Columbia.

Although the girls are given some choice in their leisure time clothes, I already knew that jeans and bermudas are not allowed, or I would have brought mine without thinking. Although they wear institution shorts for physical activities, lounging in them or anything else above the knee is not permitted. I gathered that jeans were disqualified because they tend to be tight. A senior officer explained to me that "we have to draw the line somewhere," but it seems to me that the line could be drawn a few inches above the knee rather than below and still be effective. The most clean-cut co-ed will spend her leisure time in comfortable bermudas or a snug pair of stretch pants and society approves. Yet the institution considers them "unhealthy" for the girls it is ostensibly rehabilitating to live by acceptable norms. . . . In our work uniforms we made a ragged looking group. These are old elevator operator uniforms with the sleeves ripped out and most buttons missing. They are worn over tee shirts, open to the waist and pinned from there. The officer had no more pins so I tied mine with my bathrobe sash. It struck me as inconsistent that we were allowed to be so sloppy, if comfortable, during the day but could not wear anything above the knee in the evening. . . .

Apart from being drab and unattractive, the gray skirts are very uncomfortable in warm weather. I found that the unattractive clothing induced unattractive posture. When your shirt tail is always coming out and your skirt makes you feel ten pounds heavier no matter whether you pull your stomach in or not, there seems to be no point in trying to look nice. I acquired the same slouch and sloppy walk as the other inmates through lack of incentive to look any better.

One evening a young folk singer gave a performance which the girls enjoyed tremendously. It was by far the best entertainment they had that week. When we were told after the program that he was coming over to the Center to sing some more, pandemonium broke loose. Pajamas and hair curlers disappeared in five minutes and by the time he arrived we looked and acted like ladies.

More than anything else, I missed not going outdoors often. The occasions when an extra officer was assigned to take us outside seemed to be few and far between. Some of us were allowed to sunbathe one afternoon for forty-five minutes, but we were called inside for the 3:30 count. When we asked if we could come back outside after count the officer told us we would have to ask someone higher up. The general opinion seemed to be that she was passing the buck because she knew that the officer on duty in the control room would not permit us. With a good deal of grumbling we picked up our things and went inside for the rest of the day. . . .

The girls need more exercise than most of them are getting, although their physical therapy program helps a great deal. This forty-five minutes, three days a week was sometimes shortened to half an hour when it should always be at least an hour. . . .

The food is adequate and as a rule there is enough of it. Occasionally we were short on meat which caused some grumbling. The cooks, however, showed little initiative to take extra time in preparing the food as attractively as possible. As would be expected, there is a lot of starchy food and almost no fresh fruit. There seems to be no end of candy bars and soft drinks purchased from the canteen and sometimes obtained free. During Bible class the leader treated us to coke and candy. The advantages of having some freedom in acquiring snacks are well apparent, but their choice is limited to high calory foods which too many don't need. Many of the girls expressed regret that they couldn't get more fruit, but a fruit vending machine would solve the storage problem. . . .

The weekend seemed to drag for all of the girls. On Sunday church is almost the only break in the monotony, and many girls get no satisfaction even from this.[2]

The complaint here about insufficient outside recreation is surprisingly typical. Because women's institutions are usually small, they have limited areas for physical exercise and limited staff, and these together tend to keep inmates indoors in quiet group situations that are easy to supervise. In this connection television has been universally exploited for the benefit of staff, to the detriment of prisoner health. Prisoners sitting around a TV set make up a group that is quiet, compact, easily contained, easily counted. The matron in charge likes it that way since it makes her shift go by with less effort. Of course, if there is a recreation leader on the staff she will get the girls outside to engage in soft ball or even just to sunbathe. But often a small institution will have no recreation director and even if there is one she works only the usual five shifts per week. In her absence the regular matrons feel even less responsibility for arranging physical activity other than the housekeeping chores.

[2] From an unpublished report to the District of Columbia Department of Corrections, June 1963, by Anne Keve Lindsey.

Altogether, the result is a depressing boredom, too much time to think about the rarely seen family at home, physical and mental staleness.

Training programs in women's institutions are often of little help in either relieving boredom or developing occupational skills. They tend to follow traditional lines of training for secretarial or beauty operator jobs, and it must be admitted that some institutions do offer valid training in these areas. Usually, however, these can accommodate only a few of the inmates and the rest must be content with the customary housekeeping jobs which have no training value, but are only for institutional maintenance. There has always been an assumption that women, when released, will be homemakers again and if they need any training it should mostly be in the ordinary domestic activities. So the industries in women's prisons usually tend to be such standard ones as laundries and garment shops.

To meet the needs of today's women, a far more diverse list of training opportunities must be offered. Obviously, it will be impossible to provide a good variety in a small institution, so some alternative arrangements will be essential. The most likely solution will be to utilize community resources to a greater extent than has been done until now. This is a difficult idea to sell to correctional workers as well as to the community, for there is a traditional assumption that prisoners should be imprisoned in a resolute custodial sense, surrounded by an inviolate custody perimeter. Correctional institution workers are so deeply conditioned to this that they instinctively resist any practice that does not put custody first. But wherever a more open program is tried, it becomes readily apparent that it is surprisingly workable, particularly for women prisoners, and is capable of enhancing the rehabilitative effort enormously. This affords at least a partial solution to the problem of the small women's facility.

There is increasing experience with the use of ordinary residences as annexes away from the institution. By acquiring an old house in an appropriate urban locality the institution has a place to put several of its inmates who can go to work or training programs in the community. This has mainly been attempted for work-release prisoners, but its use can well be expanded to serve those prisoners who may need to go out during the day to community resources for vocational training or special treatment and counseling services. The public's natural reaction to such experiments is that this is no way to run a prison; that this is too nice a life for a prisoner; and that the deterrent element of punishment is gone from this soft penal approach. Actually, if we must still have punishment, it is still very much here. Just ask any prisoner who has been on a work-release or study-release program. It is "hard time" to do. Having to come back to confinement every evening after being out and tasting freedom during the day is truly punishment. But hard time or not, the open, small, community-based annex offers something badly needed if we are going to pretend at all to be concerned with rehabilitation. It is the way to keep women tuned in to more normal community living which is essential to mental health, and it is important for the sake of offering counseling and vocational training opportunities in far greater variety than the typical institution could ever provide.

The "Co-ed" Institution

Careful observers of institutions believe that women prisoners have even more trouble with sexual deprivation than their male counterparts have. It may not be as readily apparent but the deprivation is real and the love affairs between women inmates are frequent and fervent. So why not a mixed-sex prison?

Some of the practical problems that would go with such a proposal are immediately obvious, but the traditional moralistic position in favor of separating the sexes is no longer respected as unthinkingly as it has been in the past. The Federal Bureau of Prisons has assumed the lead among correctional institutions in this country toward a more natural and rational practice with the recent inception of mixed-sex populations in two of its institutions. In early 1972, the bureau took over a former drug addiction treatment hospital in Fort Worth, Texas, and made it an open prison for three hundred men and about sixty women. In mid-1971, the Kennedy Youth Center, an open institution for young men in Morgantown, West Virginia, accepted sixteen young women transfers from Alderson; soon there were nearly fifty women in this recently built institution which can house three hundred or more people. It is a better than usual facility for this purpose since it consists of a number of attractive cottages scattered about a well-landscaped, open campus. The women, who range in age from sixteen to twenty-three, may be assigned to the same vocational shops where the young men are studying, but a business education course has been added for the women.

Socially the atmosphere at both the Kennedy Youth Center and the Fort Worth Correctional Institution is relaxed and natural. During free time in the evenings couples stroll about hand in hand or sit on the grass together as they would in any school. Of course, people who oppose such mixing are afraid it will go further than hand holding. Behind all the rhetoric that often is used to argue against the co-ed programming is the simple fear that girls will get pregnant. As a matter of fact it can happen. In its first year as a mixed-sex program, the Kennedy Center had one pregnancy. The bureau's attitude on this has been one of regret but not surprise or panic. They know that if the same persons were in the outside community more pregnancies than one would certainly occur, and if the same people were in one-sex institutions they would be subjected to much more distorted sex mores.

It is understandable that the first mixed-sex institution would be tried by the Federal Bureau since its facilities are more remote from any effective constituency and consequently are less vulnerable to protests. Also, most state institutions for women are much smaller and not so easily merged with other populations. However, one notable venture at the state level occurred in March 1973 when the Correctional Institution for Women at Framingham, Massachusetts, become co-ed. When its population dropped to about 85 inmates in contrast to a capacity of 150, the decision was made to place male prisoners there, relieving some of the pressure at other institutions. Two cottages now house men and two house women, with the male and female populations being of roughly equal size.

The Massachusetts experience has shown both the suitability of the idea and the difficulties of implementing it. The critics, including some dismayed and resistant staff members, predicted trouble and later circulated various embarrassing allegations. However, the institution has survived the difficult early adjustment and is now operating smoothly. Men and women mingle freely on job assignments, in recreational programs, in school classes, and in the dining room. And it works.

The situation is not without problems, but neither is a one-sex institution. Altogether, it is proving to be a rational and human way to go. It suggests that we may yet act on the thought that if the field of "corrections" is to deserve its name and not be just the field of punishment, it must have public support for the idea that people cannot be corrected or taught how to live competently in the outside community by being kept out of it and in a grossly distorted version of it. Everything we know about aiding the readjustment of people with problems argues that it must be done in the context of normal competitive social living — and of normal contact between sexes.

CHAPTER 7

Parole: Also Well Intentioned

As MUCH a part of the scene as the massive prison, and just as obsolete, is the parole board.

Not only was the prison born of the sincerest humanitarian concern, but the parole board too was conceived as a beneficent device that represented the best ideas of its time for the protection of society and the encouragement of individual reform. Nevertheless if the general public has begun to lose faith in the traditional prison, it has yet to reject the idea of the parole board.

A distinction needs to be made here between *parole* and *parole boards*. The American public has never been enthusiastic about parole, and in fact it has been a favorite whipping boy, owing to a general public impression that parolees too seldom deserve the break they have been given. This is indicative of the age-old problem that failures are always well publicized while successes are evidenced mainly by their invisibility. But the general feeling seems to be that as long as the institution of parole must exist the parole *board* is a necessity.

The original concept seemed sensible enough, and there is still much about it that is appealing. The possibility of early release could be a reward for good conduct, self-improvement, and a penitent attitude. By granting early release the state obtains the privilege of setting conditions and giving supervision in order to ensure the prisoner's stability as he reenters the community. Also, a parole decision, made at a time remote from the excited point of trial and sentencing, could be a more objective action serving to temper the harshness of the original decision.

The idea developed, too, that if a prisoner were to be released to live among the citizenry again his release should be determined by a board representative of that citizenry. Accordingly, the parole board was invented and was given the power to make awesome decisions about individual liberty and to do so in private, uninhibited by any rules of evidence or due process.

Gradually, the large number of cases has made it necessary for parole board members to work full time rather than part time as they virtually all did originally. Also, some states have accepted the view that the job calls for professional competence and cannot be left to the subjective, impressionistic approach of a lay citizen who has no sophisticated understanding of either correctional institutions or offenders. In Wisconsin, for example, the position of parole board member is a regular civil service job in the Division of Corrections. In all instances, the board members are professional people experienced in the Wisconsin correctional system, and they move by transfer or promotion to and from parole board jobs just as they would to and from other key jobs in the division.

But whether the parole board is composed of skillful professionals or lay citizens, its functioning has been a disappointing part of the correctional system, and lately the disappointment is growing. Probably the major shortcoming has been that parole board discretion is so often exercised on the basis of vaguely conceived and highly subjective criteria. Such a statement will of course be instantly denied by nearly every parole board chairman, and most of them do deserve a respectful hearing, for they are concerned and conscientious people. But the virtues of concern, conscience, and integrity are not enough. Also essential are a technique and a philosophy that are particularly relevant to the special setting of the prison and its inmates and to the more basic concepts of law. This is where the parole board idea tends to fail.

For instance, parole board members are usually good middle-class persons of undisputed and conventional moral rectitude, the kind of citizens who are indispensable to a stable and civilized society. They deserve this honest note of respect, but all too often they think their responsibility is to impose these same conventional values upon prisoners and parolees, and they communicate with the prisoners within a cultural framework that is foreign — sometimes even mystifying — to them. For instance, the parole board, in determining a prisoner's readiness for release, is usually interested in what he has done to improve himself while in prison. A prisoner may be told that his case will be continued at another hearing, six months or a year or more later, because the board wants to see him make more effort at self-improvement. That sounds virtuous enough and the public would approve this insistence that the prisoner should do more to learn a trade, finish high school, get counseling for his drinking problem, etc. But the real test of the virtue of the idea is not in the parole board's concept, but in its actual effect on the prisoner. And there the fine ethical concept comes to nothing, for the prisoner is from a different milieu, a different culture with a different set of values, and often his reaction is completely at odds with the virtuous intent of the board members.

An almost too naïve, but nevertheless actual example of this occurred in one parole board hearing which was carefully observed and reported. As a kindness, the particular state will not be mentioned, although all the members of that board have since been replaced. As the board assembled at the prison they were joined as usual by the warden, who brought with him the record of each man's chapel attendance — also as usual. The board was in a gruff mood that day and the chairman had already expressed his intention, publicly, of denying most of the parole applications because he thought there had been too many parole violators lately.

After hearing several cases and denying parole in all of them, the board encountered one young man who, they noted, had not been attending chapel lately.

"Don't you like to attend chapel?" asked the chairman.
"Yes, in fact I do," the prisoner replied.

"Then why haven't you?"

"Because I'm not a hypocrite."

"What do you mean by that?"

"Well, when I first came into this place I started attending chapel on Sundays with the other men, but then I found out that they were attending only in order to try to impress the parole board. Well I'm not a hypocrite and I don't want to look like it by being in that bunch, so I quit going to chapel."

If this prisoner thought he would, like George Washington, mitigate his punishment by being honest, he overestimated the board. He was turned down with the rest.

The illustration may be a poor one because it is out of the mainstream of the ordinary parole board approach, but in only slightly more sophisticated ways the same thing happens every day. A board typically makes it clear that the way for a man with a drinking problem to get out of prison is to have a good attendance record at the prison AA chapter. What is the effect? If that is what the parole board wants any man can develop a record of attendance at AA, the Dale Carnegie classes, a trade training or educational class. These men are often masters in the art of simulation — conning, they call it in prison.[1]

[Tragic as it is that prisoners are encouraged to simulate improvement to deceive parole boards, it is perhaps more tragic that they so often are themselves deceived in what is the true intent of the parole boards.]The deception occurs in effect despite the fact that board members invariably believe implicitly in their own rectitude. But what a board member sees as honest is not necessarily what a prisoner sees as honest. Here is the unhappy result of establishing

---

[1] "Given the acknowledged 'unnaturalness' of a prison environment, inability to assess release readiness is not surprising. The range for exercise of individual choice and responsibility is limited in today's institutions.

"Officials charged with assessing release readiness thus have meager grounds for evaluating an individual's likelihood of responsible behavior in the community. They have tended to be inclined favorably toward offenders who evidence cooperation and a 'good attitude.' But, given the institutional environment, a 'good adjustment' is not necessarily indicative of the behavior to be expected on the outside. The tendency to reward cooperation also may stem more from concern with smooth operations than from belief about its relationship to outside adjustment." *The Report on Corrections*, National Advisory Commission on Criminal Justice Standards and Goals, p. 245.

an independent board, usually of lay citizens. Because of their independent status they receive no training in understanding the special world of the prisoner and so they approach it on the basis of their usual style of relating to others, and sometimes they never learn how grossly inappropriate and counterproductive their approach actually is. Suggestions that they make, so clear in their own minds, may be vague and puzzling to the inmate. When a board resorts to the suggestion that the prisoner should "make more effort at improvement," it is likely that the advice is actually just as vague as it sounds.

But the inmates keep meticulous score on the decisions and they compare the cases that are denied with those of other men who did get parole but had not shown as much improvement as today's parole applicant who was turned down. They may further note that today's reject is a man who is a militant of some kind, a draft resister, an organizer, or merely one who likes to wear his hair and sideburns long.

Maybe the board really felt honest in saying this man needed to improve, but inmates and others who study the records are convinced that prisoners who have unorthodox life styles are told to "make a greater effort at improvement" more often than some who live more conventionally but actually may be more dangerous.

One description of the parole function from an inmate's viewpoint is provided by a recent federal prisoner. His analysis would be annoying to most parole board members, but here again it is not so important whether the analysis is right. The important thing is that this is indeed the way it appears to the inmate: "The first real purpose of parole is behavior control within the prison. Parole is the biggest prize in the prison system's grab bag. As elusive as it may be, it serves the purpose of luring prisoners into cooperation with the authorities. . . . The best descriptive term we have heard for 'progress' is what one inmate termed 'humility.' 'Humility' means that an inmate causes the authorities no trouble; it means that the inmate accepts the dictum that he is wrong and the courts and prison authorities right."[2]

    [2] Howard Levy and David Miller, *Going to Jail* (New York: Grove Press, 1971), pp. 228, 229.

The lack of professional orientation typical of most boards also shows itself in their persistent reluctance to judge cases objectively rather than subjectively. It does not matter that extensive research studies have shown that there is no relation between the length of time served and success on parole. Parole boards still cling trustingly to a feeling that certain kinds of cases should serve certain lengths of time notwithstanding good indications to the contrary.

It would not be difficult to establish a sophisticated system of criteria that would objectively determine the degree of parole risk for each case. It could simplify and speed up parole board work immeasurably. The only apparent reason this has not been done is that parole boards consistently reject anything that substitutes scientific procedure for personal bias.

This is also seen in the almost religious belief that parole boards have in the virtue and therapy of work, in their insistence that every man should have a job before being paroled. The consequence is that in almost every state thousands of days of extra time are served in prison by men who have been approved for parole but who are waiting for the uncertain help of friends or parole officers who must line up jobs for them. Here is one more contributor to hypocrisy. Someone is found who will take a chance on hiring a man whom he cannot interview and knows little about except that he is in prison; the inmate is equally in the dark about the job and the employer, but he promptly accepts the job with all the simulated signs of gratitude and agreeableness. It may be far from what he really wants, but he will readily accept it because it has become his ticket of leave. So he comes out, goes to the job, works at it a few days, and quits just as soon as he can find something more to his liking. One more employer is soured on the idea of helping ex-convicts.

Here, too, there have been studies showing that it is just as safe and usually better to parole a man without a job than for someone else to find one for him. No extra risk is involved in letting the ex-prisoner find his own job. In this way releases can be expedited and parole officers do not waste time finding jobs that may only lead to disappointments for everyone concerned. Nevertheless, most parole boards stubbornly resist the arguments and evidence. In most states the job-first principle must be served and prisoners wait extra days inside until that token job is found.

At a national conference on corrections called by the U.S. Department of Justice and held at Williamsburg, Virginia, in December 1971, the parole problem from an inmate's viewpoint was described by a general session speaker who himself was an ex-convict. He told of the prison inmates' utter frustration in trying to know what would satisfy a parole board, and he explained how the prisoners would set up their own role-playing in preparation for the ordeal. Several inmates would act the part of the parole board and inmates scheduled to meet the board would practice making their appearance, with helpful coaching from their friends. But the speaker's mournful summary to all this was that the unpredictable board always managed to defeat any rational approach that the inmates developed.

Deeply inherent in the parole board function is the problem of the vastly different vantage points of the board members and prisoner. As successful business or professional men the board members are comfortable conducting interviews in the formal setting of a board room with its big table and piles of records. They have the security of knowing the power of their position and of having their fellow members with them in the session. Self-assurance and a sense of the rightness of their function are all on their side even though uncertainty about the rightness of their individual case decisions often plagues them.

The inmate, on the other hand, comes as a supplicant, feeling intensely the psychological poverty of his position. He is by himself and essentially friendless in that room. At the same time, it is probably the moment when he is most in need of a friend, for he ordinarily is not articulate, he probably is not poised, and he may not know what points he could make in his own favor or how to shape his arguments. He is in the supremely humiliating position of having to seek a favor of several men whom he not only distrusts but often has been conditioned to hate. He is denied the self-assertive opportunity to express his dislike, and must instead feign a cordial and subservient response to questions and comments which in that kind of encounter have an abrasive effect on the supplicant even though intended as light banter by the board. As one inmate described it:

On the day appointed, the inmate dresses in his best uniform. Wistful, frightened, suspicious, sometimes sullen, but always apprehensive, he is called into the parole board meeting room. He sits or stands before the long table around which the members of the parole board are seated. His name and number are read off; his record is produced; abstracts of his case, furnished approximately two weeks before the board meets, lie before each member.

The case load at a parole board meeting may run from 50 to several hundred cases, allowing only a few minutes per inmate. "Do you think you have learned your lesson?" "Do you intend to go straight now?" "Will you behave yourself?" "Can you keep out of trouble?" "Are you sorry for what you did?" "Do you pray?" "Do you have a job?" Random questions are asked of a tense, frightened fellow who would answer almost any question in the world in whatever way he thought might get him out of the torture of his imprisonment, or safely past this critical inquisition. I am certain that all the members of the parole board ask mostly intelligent questions, but they all should realize that the answers given under such circumstances are not very credible or revealing.[3]

Even if the board decides to deny parole the prisoner is under his own inner pressure to keep a civil façade because he still has to deal with this board later if he is to get out. So he leaves the room wearing a mask of polite acceptance and only on the other side of the door can he begin to express his real feelings, made even more bitter by the necessity of concealing them from the board. His experience in the board room and his comments about it spread through the institution, fostering more hate of the parole board and adding to the dangerous tensions in the prison.

Not only does the parole hearing tend to alienate the prisoner, but it also neglects to utilize its opportunities to be constructive. This is because it excludes the prisoner from the deliberations and many if not most boards fail to give immediate decisions.

In this respect the function of the parole board goes contrary to the modern concept of behavior modification. For instance, the

[3] Verdell Sexton, Jr., in *Penal Digest International*, April–May 1972, p. 21.

"teaching machines" or programmed learning processes developed from studies by psychologist B. F. Skinner utilize his finding that a student progresses faster by being rewarded promptly whenever he gives a correct answer to a question. The reward is a very simple one; just an immediate confirmation that the answer is correct. Applied to the handling of prisoners this at least would mean that the parole board would tell the prisoner exactly what he has done that they like and don't like, exactly what decision is being made in his case and exactly why. Furthermore, this feedback would be immediate.

Altogether, this is a situation in which principles of good psychology and good law are intertwined, with both needing to be served, but instead with both being regularly violated. The legal issues involved in depriving anyone of his liberty are quite compatible with the interests of the modern therapist. Both boil down to a concern for fairness and honesty.

The Deprivation of Liberty

Our country has cherished the tradition of liberty and has been exacting about the procedures that are to be followed before depriving any individual of his freedom. Before a person may be sentenced to serve so much as a day in jail he has the right to be tried by a competent court in a public hearing; he has the right to know the evidence against him, to confront his accusers, and to be represented by counsel. But an extra day's loss of liberty at the end of the period of punishment does not seem to have the same value as a day's loss of liberty at the beginning of it. The man who could not be sentenced to jail at the time of original prosecution without all the protections of due process may later be retained in prison or summarily returned to prison from having been on parole with none of the protections that were prescribed in court. The parole board does not see itself as a judicial body, but as an administrative sentence-fixing body. As such it does not have to allow the inmate to have counsel, it does not have to hold public hearings, it does not have to give reasons for its decisions or even permit any debate on them. This freedom is justified, the argument goes, because parole is an act of grace rather than the inmate's right.

Originally, the concept was thought to be both acceptable law and good psychology. Today we must view it as neither. Gradually conditions, practices, and attitudes change, and parole boards have not fully appreciated the reality of this change. What was once an act of grace is now a right, and freedom — whether the freedom of a nonoffending free citizen or that of a parolee — is in either case a privilege not to be dealt with lightly. However, the fact is that many men are behind bars because of noncriminal and even unproved activity that was annoying to parole boards rather than actually illegal in nature. This was originally part of a respected concept. The Wickersham Commission of 1931 noted this feature of parole in language that revealed its fervent acceptance of the idea: "The parolee will find himself continuously under the eyes of the State. Society need not wait until he is convicted for the commission of another crime in order to lock him up again. The slightest deviation from the straight and narrow path will bring him back within the prison walls. Parole may be a method of punishment, but more than that, it is a method of prevention second to none."

The intent was a noble one, to watch the parolee's conduct and bring him back into custody whenever he might violate rules which the parole board thought important. It was an honest effort to keep the parolee from new criminal activity. But in today's context the suspicion arises that a parolee's liberty may be lost not because of an offense, but because he may fail to maintain the life style considered impeccable by certain middle-class persons who are parole board members.

It hardly matters whether this is in fact true. The damage is done by the parolee's belief that it is true, and this belief is heavily supported by the character of parole board decision making, especially in respect to parole revocations. For instance, in California in recent years about one-fourth of all admissions to state prisons are parolees being returned without new convictions. As one observer has reported on the administrative revocation hearings,

The accused gets fifteen or twenty minutes alone with a clerk and two hearing representatives who vacillate among the roles of prosecuting attorney, sentencing judge and prison classification committee.

There are no spectators, no witnesses, no counsel, no competent evidence; even the hearsay evidence, usually an investigative report by the parole agent and sometimes a police report, is often meager on facts and specifics and the agent is not present to supply missing links or answer questions. The function of the hearing officers, after an often very casual finding that the parolee is guilty of the allegations against him, is to determine whether or not this misconduct warrants imprisonment, a decision as to which the original judicial commitment obviously had nothing to do.[4]

Under such conditions it has been known for a parolee to be tried in court for a new offense, to be acquitted of it, but still to be brought back to the prison as a violator because of the parole board's suspicion that he probably was guilty anyway.

The Parole Contract

A recent and much discussed innovation is the parole contract, a device intended to supply more incentive and fairness in the parole decision-making process. The idea received a major push in 1972 when the American Correctional Association started a project known as the Mutual Agreement Program (MAP). The initial impact resulted in adaptations of the idea in Wisconsin, Arizona, and California, and other states since then have been experimenting with their own versions.

The essential feature of the concept is that the parole board determines for each individual case what specific things should be expected of the inmate as prerequisite to parole. He may be required to take a prescribed number of hours of drug or alcohol counseling or a prescribed trade training course, or to complete his high school education. These or any other conditions considered important in his case would be discussed with him and would be subject to mutual agreement, resulting in a contract which would commit the parole board to grant release on the inmate's completion of the contracted requirements.

[4] Caleb Foote. "A Program for Prison Reform in the United States." Final report of the Annual Chief Justice Earl Warren Conference on Advocacy, June 1972. Sponsored by the Roscoe Pound American Trial Lawyers Foundation, Cambridge, Massachusetts. P. 21.

The original presumption in the MAP planning was that the contract would be legally binding, but this is an idea that parole boards find difficult to accept, since it threatens to limit their discretion. In Minnesota the approach has been to experiment with a "specific performance agreement," and the understanding is that the parole board has a strong moral obligation to honor the agreement, but is not legally bound.

So far there seems to be no assumption that the parole contract can be used with all inmates. It is difficult to adapt it to the inmate with a long sentence or to the volatile, unstable, assaultive prisoner. Probably it will also be ineffective with the mentally ill or severely emotionally disturbed inmate. A further problem is that it will require extra staff time to administer.

With all the problems and uncertainties about it, the parole contract does offer for some inmates a helpful incentive and relief from uncertainty, and for those inmates it means a more reasonable and constructive prison experience. The impact of the idea on the total correctional scene is minuscule so far, but it is very much worth some persistent and thoughtful experimenting.

Adapting to Noninstitutional Programs

When the parole idea developed and became widespread in the early years of the twentieth century, the correctional options were few and simple. A convicted offender could be at large on probation, or he could be in prison. The advent of parole introduced a new option, but it was essentially no different from probation in permitting the offender to live at large in the community under supervision. The parole board decision was just a matter of deciding whether the prisoner should be inside or out. Furthermore, these simple, clear-cut distinctions between inside the institution and outside on probation or parole have often been reinforced by their organizational separateness. In many instances probation services and parole services and institutions have been administered so separately that there has been no sharing between them even of important case information.

But a significant and very substantial change is occurring in this respect. There is a new concern about having the field services (probation and parole) and the institutional programs closely coordinated and more unified in a joint effort to correct their clients. As a result, new programs are developing that combine features of both the institutional and the field services, blurring the distinctions between them and calling for new processes of handling cases. Examples are pre-release centers, work-release programs, weekend furloughs, and certain halfway houses. A likely new development will be the prison annex, a separate house, perhaps away from the prison but technically a part of the institution and an "extension of the limits of confinement." It may work best if it can be treated as part of the prison, enabling some inmates to be transferred to it if the staff so decides. But will the parole board be able to adapt to a correctional program which makes some rather different philosophical demands upon board members?

These are developments that strain the traditional concept of the parole board's function and unless the particular board is unusually flexible the new programs are handicapped substantially. The typical outcome is that the program and its clients must adapt to standard parole board procedures rather than expect the board to adapt to new program designs.

The new community-based self-help programs may be staffed by ex-offenders, nonconformists, etc., who often are vexatious to parole boards, for an almost standard provision in state parole policies forbids a parolee to associate with other parolees or other convicted offenders. Although this is gradually being liberalized, at least thirty-three states still retain this parole rule. This ranges from Alabama's vague admonition "not [to] associate with persons of bad reputation or harmful character" to New York's more explicit ban on association with "any individual having a criminal record." These restrictions exist despite the discovery that a potent source of assistance is the self-help group which calls for the deliberate association of former offenders in a dynamic and constructive effort to improve themselves.

Obviously, some parole boards are ignoring their own rules enough to permit the parolee's involvement in self-help groups, but by no means is this always so. In California both parole and corrections officials were stoutly opposed to the involvement of parolees in the Synanon program for all the years of its early development. Synanon had been studied by outside observers and books had been written on its unique effectiveness in helping drug addicts, but for years California parolees with drug problems were restricted by intransigent parole rules and forbidden to use Synanon.

Parole boards have always shown a remarkable naïveté about the world of the parolee, undoubtedly reflecting the very conventional middle-class orientation of most board members. Often the repeat offender is a person who lives in a culture where the occasional breaking of laws, perhaps by his own family members and close friends, is very common. Yet he is just as dependent upon his family and his group of culturally homogeneous intimates as the middle-class person is upon his group. So the state takes this offender and for a period of time forces him to associate even more with persons of ill repute; forces him to live in a cell block with perhaps several hundred of them for a few years and then suddenly demands that he accept a complete reversal of this condition. He is to leave the exclusive company of felons, return to the community, and somehow live happily with new people whom he has not known before and who have different tastes and interests, avoiding any regular contact with familiar friends who may have at some time been in trouble with the law.

It is a singularly unrealistic demand which practically guarantees an early parole violation unless the parole board denies the importance or honesty of its own rule. Undoubtedly, the rules are often bent in the face of reality, but just as undoubtedly the strictly interpreted parole rule sends many parolees back to prison without having committed any new offenses. Frequently it means that a man is imprisoned for merely persisting in his own life style. The ease with which this can happen is suggested by the agreement that a New York parolee must sign.

I will lead a law abiding life and will conduct myself as a good citizen. I understand that this means I must not associate with evil companions or any individual having a criminal record; that I must avoid questionable resorts, abstain from wrongdoing, lead an honest, upright and industrious life, support my dependents, if any, and assume towards them all my moral and legal obligations, and that my behavior must not be a menace to the safety of my family or to any individual or group of individuals.

And this is only one of the sixteen conditions of parole that he must accept.

In the face of this deeply entrenched belief in the virtue of the conventional rules of conventional life styles, the treatment programs that bring ex-offenders together are only grudgingly accepted by parole boards. It seems odd that the principle involved in the Alcoholics Anonymous program can be so accepted there but not in other groups. The AA organization brings alcoholics together in a dynamic self-help program. But even though Synanon and some other groups have demonstrated the utility of putting ex-offenders together for similar effect, it is an idea that many parole boards find offensive and quite unacceptable. So the parole rules promote hypocrisy, with the prison inmate signing an agreement which he cannot possibly meet and the parole board either bringing parolees back for picayune reasons or else avoiding enforcement of the rules.

The fact that parole boards do imprison many parolees just for violating the rules, coupled with the unrestricted decision-making freedom enjoyed by parole boards, explains why it is generally thought that parole, which was designed as a means to shorten time served, has instead been subverted to a function of increasing time served.

The task of improving parole board structure and practice will be a difficult one to accomplish in view of the entrenched biases and the complex legal and political issues involved. For the most part substantial changes cannot be made unless they are also made in statutory penalties, sentencing procedures, correctional administrative structures, and related field services. But one of the improvements that could be made immediately is perhaps one of the most important, and that is to start shaping parole board procedures for more constructive effect upon inmates, rather than for administrative convenience.

Of first importance is the need to deal with each inmate with a quality of honesty that actually comes across to the inmate as honesty rather than satisfying only the board members themselves in this respect. This quality of honesty will, for example, require that a parole board share with the inmate all case information that is available to the board; that it all be discussed fully in the inmate's presence; that the inmate listen to the subsequent discussion leading to a decision in his case; that he in this way receive knowledge of the board's decision before leaving the hearing room.

Because a suggestion of this sort will be anathema to most parole boards, it might be useful to consider the arguments they would most certainly advance against it. A major issue is the confidentiality of records: reports of psychiatrists and other clinicians have always been written and submitted only for the use of staff; in some cases certain information, if shared with the inmate, would jeopardize the safety of other persons.

In answer to this highly traditional position it must be said that, of course, a clinical report that was written in confidence should not be disclosed to the inmate. But as soon as the board decides to share case information with the inmate, the clinicians are immediately told of this and therefore can prepare their reports with this in mind. There is no ethical problem of confidentiality if every contributor of information to the file knows that his information will be shared. This gives him the chance to withhold it or to reshape it with disclosure in mind.

To the average parole board this may seem a painfully radical notion, but ten or fifteen years ago the idea was just as painful to courts and probation officers in respect to the presentence report. Probation offices had always been just as steeped in the tradition of strict confidentiality of case material, and offered the same argument that disclosure of the presentence report would dry up their information sources. But a quiet revolution took place and as more and more probation offices were subjected to the practice of disclosing reports they found that they could still function professionally and that in fact there were some unanticipated benefits. When the officer knows that his report will be scrutinized and possibly challenged, he is more careful to construct his case with professional care and objectivity.

The result of disclosure has been better case reporting instead of the crippling effect that had been feared.

There may sometimes be basis for the argument that the safety of some other person may be jeopardized if certain pieces of information are disclosed. The Federal Parole Board is especially concerned with this in certain cases involving organized crime. But the validity of this argument is probably reduced considerably by the fact that prisoners usually have more information or more accurate surmises than parole boards give them credit for. Grapevines are more energetic purveyors of information than official channels are. Though it could never be proved, it may easily be that more retaliatory acts have been undertaken on the basis of withheld or distorted information than would ever have been prompted by official and accurate information.

The parole board's preference for discussing a case outside the prisoner's hearing is entirely understandable and natural. It simply is much more comfortable to be able to talk in unguarded privacy. In fact, the feeling goes beyond a matter of comfort to become a concern for personal safety. Board members are not eager to incur the wrath of an inmate by having him know of their individual votes against his parole. But, of course, they find more elegantly framed arguments to support their exclusion of the inmate from their deliberations.

There has been far too little appreciation of the therapy of honesty — as well as its feasibility. When a competent board deliberates a case they carefully weigh both positive and negative factors; the negative ones are considered in the context of what is best for the inmate himself; the positive factors are presented sincerely in a concern for an honestly balanced picture. It is a workmanlike procedure leading to a rational and sound conclusion — if we may assume it to be a professionally conscientious board. But if the inmate is not present and the vote is to deny parole, he is, by his exclusion, granted license to imagine the sorriest kind of board process. He has no idea of the professional quality of the deliberations; he has no guess that certain board members spoke very positively of him; he gets no feel of what the board is really expecting of him. Even if the decision has been to grant parole, the inmate, and other inmates who try to analyze it, has only murky concepts of what criteria the board used, if indeed the decision was made on more than a whimsical basis. And so by excluding the inmate from deliberations, the board actually encourages and perpetuates the inmates' resentment and contributes to poor prison morale.

In many states, and with the Federal Parole Board, the major impediment to including the inmate in the discussions and decision-making process is the enormous volume of cases. (California's parole board, the California Adult Authority, must make from 2500 to 3000 decisions per month.) Some boards, to keep from becoming far too large, use referees or hearing representatives who travel to the institutions, hold brief interviews with inmates, and later meet with the board to discuss the case and arrive at a decision. In such situations, inmates consistently and bitterly describe the superficial ten-minute interviews after which they have to wait perhaps six weeks for a slip of paper which tells the decision, but does not give the reasons.

Admittedly the demands of high case volume make it exceedingly difficult to treat each case with the deliberate consideration that it deserves, but with innovations such as some of those enumerated on the following pages we should be able to reduce the problem considerably. What has been lacking is the motivation to design and implement a better way, and this is only because parole boards and legislatures have been largely oblivious to the inmates' viewpoint and the damaging effects the usual decision-making process has on them.

Sharing information and deliberations with the inmates is a step that most parole boards could make immediately if they cared to. There are still other steps they could take to improve the process if they wished to develop the administrative means. Ideally, for instance, an inmate would be given notice about two weeks to a month before the exact day and time of his parole hearing and then he would have the privilege of inviting as many as three or four other persons to sit with him and participate in the hearing. This might include his wife or parents, his minister, or a lawyer. The family to which a man is returning is exceedingly important to the parole plan and the board may be helped materially in its decision by actually seeing and talking with family members.

The issue of permitting legal representation in board hearings is a lively one. Every board gets frequent requests for a lawyer to be present, and most boards have not so far permitted it. It is in this issue that they come closest to admitting that board policy is based on administrative convenience. There is fear of "opening the door"; fear that requests for legal representation would be excessive, would require much more board time, and that sooner or later indigent inmates would have to be accorded legal services if they requested them.

Certainly all these are possibilities, as is the notion that some day the controversy will have to be resolved on the basis of what is right instead of on the basis of administrative convenience. When the day comes that we decide to follow good principle instead of administrative feasibility we will find ways to accommodate the extra demands of good principle.

Probably there is no way to design a release procedure which would guarantee the most constructive handling of each inmate's case, the most positive impact on prison populations, and the most protection for society. We will always be subject to the vagaries of human nature and man's inadequacy to deal with the complexities of his own institutions. Furthermore, there will always be great differences in the conditions and needs of widely diverse states. But some important principles are evident and from them a fundamental model can be suggested. It should include such elements as the following.

1. *Parole board members should be full time and should be given extensive training in interview techniques, law, sociology, and psychology as these relate to parole board functioning.*

Such training should be required for each new board member before he assumes his duties and whether or not he has had previous professional experience or training. The training should be the responsibility of an appropriate university and it should include periodic refresher training sessions. It should also include direct and thorough presentations by ex-prison inmates.

2. *In populous states the case decisions should be made by parole board representatives while the board itself functions mainly to determine policy.*

To combat the inexorable problem of overwhelming case loads and to keep a parole board from becoming unwieldy in size, it would be best to keep the board small and to limit its function to administration and policy setting, except for occasional case decisions as described below.

3. *Cases should be objectively classified for different levels of handling.*

It is quite possible for any state to establish a list of criteria which would serve to classify cases according to the type of parole board processing they should receive. Presently, boards follow the same hearing and decision-making process for all cases. It would be more efficient if cases were categorized according to certain case characteristics that have predictive value and given differential handling according to the needs of each. Then a few would receive full-scale board hearings while most others could be disposed of with much less time involved. This idea is developed further in the following points.

4. *Parole board representatives should individually hear and decide cases.*

As already noted, the assistance gained by a parole board in having representatives go out and hear cases for them is partly defeated by the need for the representatives to reach a decision in conference with the board. There seems to be a notion that a parole decision cannot be made by just one person, which overlooks the fact that the original sentence was made in court by one judge.

Of course, there is a bit more safety in a joint decision by three or more persons, but that simply is a luxury we can no longer afford. The disadvantages inherent in the delays it causes now outweigh its additional assurance of safety.

If a parole board will accept the foregoing point 3 and work out a system of case categories, it can operate safely enough with three levels of decision making such as the following.

a. According to standard objective criteria, the majority of cases would be classified for hearing and decision by a board representative. This would mean that, subject to policies established by the board, a representative would by himself hear all cases in this category and reach an immediate decision on each one.

b. The second category of cases would be those that have some extra sensitive quality that calls for a sharing of the decision. In these cases the hearing representative would interview the prisoner as usual but would, as now, go back to the board to have his opinion ratified or not by at least two other members of the board. Better, if the necessary logistics can be developed, these cases might be bunched for hearing at the same time and the two board members could accompany the representative to the institution at that less frequent time. In this way these cases too would be decided on immediately.

c. A third category of cases would be those few which are of such notoriety or which present such special danger that they require consideration by the full board. Here too it would be desirable for the board to interview the inmate in person and arrive at its decision then and there.

This system of using three categories and permitting a single representative to make his own decision in cases of the first category will work well or not depending upon the courage of the parole board in fashioning the categories in the first place. If the board is timid and reserves most cases for the second and third categories the plan will be no solution at all.

5. All case data should be subject to challenge.

This point has some extensive implications when considered in a broad sense. It is quite common, for instance, that disciplinary reports are written impulsively by guards and, whether or not any action is taken on them, they are placed in the case file and sometimes become surprisingly incriminating in their effect. It may be years later at a parole hearing that a board member will leaf through a file and note disciplinary reports as if they were fresh infractions, even though other people had long since forgotten the events. It is seldom realized how much sense of injustice this kind of record provokes in an already hostile inmate.

So this rule should first of all mean that no disciplinary report should ever go into an inmate file unless the inmate has a copy and an opportunity to challenge it. Even if the misconduct charge is found valid and punishment is ordered, such charges should be excluded from any permanent file if they are infrequent or minor. An inmate should have the right not to be jeopardized by misbehavior that he has left in the past.

In support of this argument is the fact that many incidences of misconduct in a prison are peculiar to the prison setting which provokes personal instances of rebellion against the depersonalization of the system. Record of these should not be preserved in the file for later use by a parole board which fails to see that some kinds of minor misconduct in the prison may have no reliable bearing on the prisoner's capacity for successful adjustment on the outside.

This point also means that every bit of case data accessible to the parole board should be accessible to the inmate as well. Of course, even if a parole board were to agree to this idea wholeheartedly there would still be forbidding logistical problems to overcome. Nevertheless, the technology is available to do it and because of the crucial demands of basic fairness it should be a priority item for every board. The board should be supplied with a standard document on the case, and the inmate would have a copy of the same.[5] To make effective the opportunity of challenge, the inmate should get the document a few days in advance of the hearing, soon enough to let it influence him in his choice of the several people whom he would be privileged to have at his side in the hearing.

6. *In a majority of cases a fixed date of parole should be established at the first hearing.*

It may be that this approach should be taken only with the previously suggested category of cases which can be handled fully

[5] It is often stated that parole boards need more case data than they have in order to make more intelligent decisions. It is argued here, however, that perhaps boards usually have too much information instead of too little. The thick case file with its vast accumulation of material hides as well as reveals. The board would be better served by a streamlined single document that would summarize those items of information that have been identified by good research as having pertinence to the decision-making process.

by parole board representatives. In these cases of lesser public threat it would fit very well with recent trends in treatment techniques to give a new prisoner a specific release date and to assure him that he will be freed on that date without further hearing and without regard to what his behavior is in the meantime. (The privilege of permitting an earlier release date for especially meritorious conduct should be retained.) It is a radical idea and quite opposite from the venerable philosophy of making a man earn his release. Yet it is beginning to gain some respectful recognition and is certain to become more favorably regarded in the future.

Support for the idea has recently come from an unexpected source which frames the argument quite competently. The General Assembly of the United Presbyterian Church, in its annual meeting, May 1972, adopted an extensive position paper on correctional matters which dealt in part with this issue.

Individuals sentenced to institutional care and custody shall, within ninety days of admission, be given a definite release date based exclusively upon the nature of the offense and the pattern of the offender's criminal history.

A variety of sentencing and paroling methods has evolved that places increased emphasis upon discretion on the part of the paroling authority and upon indefiniteness, even indeterminancy, regarding the length of an offender's period of confinement. Such indefiniteness has increasingly been used in forcing involvement with dubious treatment objectives, in prolonging the confinement of nonconforming inmates, and in rewarding inmates who have served questionable institutional purposes. It has also become cruelly destructive to the human spirit as it deprives the prisoner of a time-frame within which he can hope and prepare for his future. Therefore, a definite release date should be made known to the offender within ninety days of admission, and confinement beyond that date should not be permitted irrespective of the prisoner's involvement in programs, his disciplinary records, or his political activities. Should periodic review reveal a demonstrative readiness on the part of the prisoner for successful reintegration into the community, the originally stipulated period of confinement may be shortened by the paroling authority and an earlier guaranteed release date established and made known to the prisoner.[6]

6 *Social Deliverances*, 184th General Assembly, the United Presbyterian Church in the United States of America, Denver, Colorado, May 16–24, 1972, p. 10.

Further discussion of the treatment concepts involved in this argument will be found in chapter 9.

A model such as the foregoing would certainly need extensive modifications from state to state. Nor would it be a panacea everywhere. A very poor system run by humane and perceptive people will serve its clientele much better than an ideal system under indifferent leadership, but the parole board concept is deeply in need of change and if the model above is not the shape of the future at least it can contribute to the search for the release procedure that will better meet the need.

CHAPTER 8

Prisoners Discover the Law

TWENTY YEARS AGO a federal prisoner at the U.S. Penitentiary in Leavenworth, Kansas, was denied his request to deal directly with the U.S. Patent Office in processing an invention he had developed. Policies of the Bureau of Prisons required that such an effort was subject to bureau approval, and so he could deal with the Patent Office only through the Bureau of Prisons headquarters.

The prisoner took the matter to court, but received no comfort from that source. In June 1954, the U.S. 10th Circuit Court of Appeals ruled in his case that "courts are without power to supervise prison administration or to interfere with ordinary prison rules or regulations." The court's supreme certainty of the orthodoxy of its view was underscored in its final comment in the case: "No authorities are needed to support those statements. The appeal is wholly without merit."[1]

The decision did indeed reflect the general view of courts which had long before drifted into a comfortable acceptance of the dogma that there was no authority for court interference in the internal affairs of a prison. The roots of the idea are found in much earlier and somewhat self-righteous attitudes of the public and the

[1] Banning v. Looney, 213, F2d, 771.

courts, which hold that the prisoner, who could perhaps have been put to death by society, or at least given a longer prison term, should actually be grateful that his lot was not worse. A quite typical expression of this attitude was a Virginia court's pronouncement in 1891 that "the prisoner, as a consequence of his crime, not only forfeited his liberty but all his personal rights except those which the law in its humanity accords to him. He is for the time being the slave of the state."[2]

With such a prevailing mood, it could hardly be expected that courts would feel any need to review the internal affairs of a prison. When courts nevertheless were urged to consider prison problems on occasion, other common rationalizations were found to support judicial noninvolvement. It could be argued that courts lacked the prerequisite knowledge of prison administration, and that any judicial interference would tend to undermine authority and control in the prison. Altogether such arguments were sufficiently appealing to the courts to result in a well-established "hands-off" philosophy regarding internal prison complaints. But in the 1940s signs of change began to appear and one court decision emerged in 1944 which was radical in comparison with prevailing views, though its great significance was little appreciated at the time. The 6th U.S. Circuit Court of Appeals stated simply, "A prisoner retains all the rights of an ordinary citizen except those expressly, or by necessary implication taken from him by law."[3]

Though overlooked for some years, the meaning of that basic declaration appeared with fascinating suddenness during the sixties as one court after another accepted cases regarding the treatment of prisoners and ruled on pertinent details of prison management. It was a startling development that brought not only new concerns to prison administrators, but a new role to attorneys.

With the changed attitude on the part of the courts, the field of criminal law has caught the interest of aggressive young lawyers who find in it an exciting opportunity for effective attack on a neglected social problem. It is an inevitable and integral aspect of the

[2] Ruffin v. Commonwealth, 62 Va., 21 Drott 790, 796 (1891).
[3] Coffin v. Reichard, 143, F2d, 443.

widespread disillusionment with the establishment on the part of a militant generation eager to force social improvement. Thousands of young people had been miserably frustrated in their efforts to hasten U.S. withdrawal from Vietnam or to change many of the other defects they saw in the system around them. But at least those who were coming out of law school and entering the new legal services agencies found that a big social challenge existed right among them in our penal system, and its vulnerability to legal attack was clear and explicit.

Quite naturally this confluence of events has brought some exceedingly unsettling experiences for a few prison administrators, specific situational improvements for a few prisoners, and altogether the most viable leverage for prison amelioration that has appeared lately.

It is fully appropriate to refer to this more as a promise than as an accomplished means of prison reform, for as yet very few court actions have taken place in comparison with the vast potential for such actions. Furthermore, we can expect in the future an intense judicial probing of prison operation and philosophy that may go far beyond the relatively light touch that the courts have used so far.

At this point prison administrators are reacting to the court decisions with approval only in rare cases, more often with feelings that range from mild annoyance to anger. Much of the time their reaction is like that of any person who finds someone else telling him how to do his job. It becomes particularly galling for administrators when the court provides highly detailed instructions about specific prison procedures, stripping the warden of his accustomed privilege of setting the prison practices as he sees fit.

A proper perspective on the matter must recognize that it is indeed a handicap to the warden to have his administrative options interfered with; but the hard truth is that court intervention in the general operation of prisons is now here to stay, partly because some of the custodians, by abuse of their options, have themselves made it necessary, and just as often because the public has so miserably supported the whole criminal justice system that its administrators could not possibly operate it with true humaneness. For example, minimal salaries for guards and lack of budgets for training inevitably foster tense, and often outright destructive, staff-inmate relationships. There is no necessity to suggest that the abuse or neglect of prisoners has been deliberate. No matter how honest and well meaning an administration is, the insensitive procedures or the deteriorated and overcrowded buildings are as hurtful in effect as if hurt were intended.

Of course, the process of change and of adapting to new rules of the game is painful, as the police discovered when courts began specifying new guidelines for arrest and investigation procedures. As yet, both the lawyers and the prison administrators are learning how to adjust to court intervention, and there is at times an inefficient spinning of wheels. Occasionally prison administrators react with bad humor and gross uncooperativeness to the incursion of the legal profession into prison affairs when actually the possible court actions have potential for helping the warden. Some court decisions, for instance, may mandate certain budget improvements that the warden has made futile efforts to get.

A warden may be able to see and appreciate this intellectually, but there is an emotional component in the situation that sometimes overrides the rational view. Court processes, being adversary in nature, tend to produce lengthy written allegations which at times seem to say that the warden is himself cruel, callous, neglectful. The warden, not being a lawyer and not being inured to this standard legal approach, is likely to be furious at the implication that his prison reflects his idea of how it should be rather than the fact that it is an outdated, unworkable physical plant which he cannot replace, but must operate with a budget that does not permit him to train his staff properly or even to hire enough staff to control and protect his prisoners from one another.

Lawyers too will gradually learn to select and construct their suits with more telling effect and less wasted effort. There have in recent years been elaborate actions started by attorneys who failed to understand the complexity of prison management problems, or the elusive character of intangible conditions which are most difficult to encompass in traditional legal language. The result has been that wardens have fretted for hours in preparing answers to interrogatories, only to see the ponderous action fizzle out and end in no action at all.

The warden of one large city jail was sued by an inmate who charged that the segregation cell in which he was held for punishment purposes was in such bad condition that it constituted cruel and unusual punishment. The warden, himself unhesitatingly critical of his outworn and overcrowded jail, was inclined to agree with the allegation, but he did not see the sense in taking time from his regular work to write a response to an interrogatory that contained a total of forty-eight questions, all of which called for some painstaking accumulation of data, much of it quite irrelevant to the real issue of how to get a new jail and an adequate operating budget.

In another case the same warden was sued for multiple alleged injustices, a few of which were related to the jail ("forced to live in a dangerous, unfit and overcrowded jail cell") but more of which were conditions entirely outside the warden's jurisdiction ("denied the right to take a lie detector test, and subjected to four line-ups"). This is a common feature of prisoners' suits, and an obvious cause of resentment by already overburdened administrators who tend to react to the immediate problems presented by such suits instead of seeing them in broader perspective.

But despite all the wasteful motion and the legal actions which end ineffectively, some legal actions are clearly relevant and produce equally clear-cut and sensible effects. An outstanding example was a Rhode Island case in 1970 regarding the censorship of prisoners' mail.[4] As in most states, the prisons in Rhode Island had for decades followed the traditional practices on censorship of mail with rules that were multiple and detailed. For example: "Incoming mail must not exceed two sheets, and cannot be larger than 8½ inches by 11 inches in size." The typical fear of criticism was explicit in the rules about the contents of outgoing letters: "Correspondence must contain information of a personal nature to you and your correspondent only. It must not contain information about or from other

4 Palmigiano v. Travisono, 317 F. Supp. 776.

inmates, discussion of institutional problems of policies or reference to institutional personnel."

The court not only rejected the need to forbid such criticism, but also was unimpressed with the concern of the prison administrators that prisoners might write nuisance letters. This has been a standard argument in support of censorship as long as there have been prisons, but the court disposed of this issue in a brief and sharp comment. "Officials of the Adult Correctional Institution have also taken it upon themselves to read and screen outgoing mail to protect the public, including the courts, from insulting, vulgar letters. This is not their function — they are not the protectors of the public which can protect itself."

The court essentially ended the censorship of prison mail in Rhode Island with this declaration: "The reading of any outgoing mail from the inmates is unnecessary and in violation of the First Amendment rights of the parties involved unless pursuant to a duly obtained search warrant, and in the absence of the same no outgoing prisoner mail may be opened, read or inspected."

Court actions of this kind may take prisons well beyond the immediate changes or action they require, for they force administrators to discover that the prison can still operate even if hallowed concepts are laid aside. Quite possibly the best effect of such court actions will be to help loosen up the tradition-bound world of prisons and make the custodians at all levels generally more receptive to ideas for change.

Disciplinary practices used by prison management have also come under legal attack. The time is especially ripe for such attack since prisons are receiving more of the "political" prisoners, who have a talent for inviting punishment. This should surprise no one, for the militant and articulate iconoclast is a prisoner who outrages the custodians, partly for ideological reasons and partly because he so clearly uses his leadership qualities to threaten the security of the prison. Prison officials, being quite human, react emotionally to the militant, for he is very different in his misbehavior from the more ordinary convict. He is more openly defiant and with his good intelligence and great sense of mission he finds persistent and exasperating ways to goad the custodians into overreaction. His is not the furtive misbehavior of the old con who is caught fermenting raisins under some backstairs. His instead is an open challenge of the system, and the custodians assume instinctively that a bold challenge must be decisively suppressed or they risk losing control of the whole prison population. Unlike the familiar old con who accomplishes his purpose when he keeps his mischief undetected, the militant will accomplish his purpose only when he is caught and overly punished, for then he has legal grounds for defeating the system. Since the custodians often fail to realize what the ideological militant is doing, he tends to receive more heavy-handed punishment from prison disciplinary committees and more extensions of time from parole boards. Even other prisoners resent it when the persons being punished or denied parole are not criminally dangerous outside, but only protestors against unpopular laws.

Administering punishment within prisons has historically been very much at the discretion of the prison staffs and in no way subject to review. In extreme examples the result has been a savage brutality which has failed to shock the American conscience as much as it should, partly because it has been so excessively vicious that the public has not been inclined to believe that it would actually happen in this time in this country. The details of prisoner mistreatment have been richly described in documents that relatively few people read.

Even now, when gross physical abuse is infrequent, and when prison disciplinary committees are trying conscientiously to handle misbehavior sensibly, subtle forms of unfairness easily creep in. The due process concepts that are avidly protected until an offender is convicted are essentially unknown in prison. And yet the arbitrary and unreviewable actions of a disciplinary committee may have a material effect upon the time a man serves. This may occur either through a decision to forfeit his "good time" or through some accusatory entry in the case file which will affect later parole board decisions.

The arbitrariness of internal disciplinary actions has been a cause of poor prison morale far beyond the realization of most custodians. So it was a surprise and a shock to many prison administrators in 1970 when a federal court in Rhode Island defined in elaborate detail the administrative procedures that would have to be followed to classify prisoners and to determine disciplinary measures.[5] The complaint was that both classification and disciplinary actions were based on vague criteria and handled unsystematically. Going farther than any previous court action had ventured, this court order set forth explicitly the definitions of each classification category and the procedures to be observed at all steps of the disciplinary process. Furthermore, the court retained jurisdiction for eighteen months in order to review directly and continually the conduct of the revised procedures during that time.

Only two months following the Rhode Island case a federal court in New York acted on the plea of a militant prisoner who had been placed in segregation with greatly restricted privileges mainly because his activities were defiant in quality rather than actual violations of clear and valid rules.[6] Here again the court's action essentially was to insist on the elements of due process — the furnishing of a written copy of charges, a recorded hearing with opportunity for representation, and the furnishing of a written decision on the disciplinary action. The court also specified that the extended period of segregation and the deprivation of physical comforts and communication were cruel beyond necessity. The prisoner was granted damages for each day he was in segregation and his lost good time was ordered restored.

An area of concern that may have still more significance for the future of corrections is the growing court interest in the quality of prison rehabilitation efforts. When no one expected prisons to do more than punish people this was no issue; but now that there is expectation of offering treatment there is an accompanying expectation that if a prison claims intent or capability to treat, then it should in fact provide real treatment. This is a qualitative area which presents the court with the imposing task of identifying just what is valid

[5] Morris v. Travisono, 310 F. Supp. 857 (D.R.I. 1970).
[6] Sostre v. Rockefeller, 312 F. Supp. 863 (S.D.N.Y. 1970).

treatment — a difficult enough task for the clinicians themselves. Nevertheless, the issue was faced by a circuit court in Maryland which had before it, in 1971, a suit filed by inmates of the Patuxent Institution for Defective Delinquents. Though this facility was created to treat chronic and compulsive lawbreakers, its physical design has the same custodial features as any prison, and it resorted to the occasional use of the usual isolation cells for punitive segregation.

The petitioners contended that they were confined in isolation cells for prolonged time periods, that the cells were unlighted and dirty, that toilets could be flushed only by a guard in the corridor but that guards were not regularly present, and that confinement was continuous except when they were released once a week to take a shower.

In addition to hearing numerous witnesses in the courtroom, the court took a day-long tour of the institution to observe conditions firsthand. The segregation cells were defended by a psychiatrist at the institution as being compatible with the overall treatment effort, being "negative reinforcers." But the court in its findings stated, "The Court is of the opinion that they are not, as practiced at Patuxent Institution, negative reinforcements, and has found from the voluminous testimony of many witnesses that they are contrary to the rehabilitation of the inmates and serve no therapeutic value of any kind. They are, in fact, methodology adopted by the custodial staff to better maintain order within the institution."[7]

Although we in corrections have talked fondly of giving treatment and of the desirability of using correctional officers much more than we have in counseling roles, here was an instance of a court being the aggressive agent in this respect and prodding the corrections staff into living up to its own beliefs.

It is the opinion of this Court that Patuxent Institution . . . has been ineffectual in developing or providing the specialized treatment attention which defective delinquents require, and experience has indicated that this will continue until the institution has developed

[7] McCray v. Maryland, in the Circuit Court for Montgomery County, Maryland. Decided November 11, 1971.

more effective programs in the area of training of its administrative and custodial staff. The Court feels that the professional staff, in light of such programs, could instill a dedication and a determination in the correctional officer to help patients rehabilitate themselves, thus re-establishing the good faith and human concern required within the institution between patient and staff.[8]

As a result of the suit the court established explicit rules governing all details of segregation practices.

Reference was made in the beginning of this chapter to early court decisions which rejected pleas from prisoners because they had no right to complain. It is heartening to note, by contrast, a recent court case in which a three-judge court gave the most careful attention to a group of prisoner plaintiffs who were not so much challenging specific abusive acts as they were complaining that "conditions in the prisons violate rights guaranteed to the prisoners by the Constitution and laws of the United States and the Constitution and laws of the Commonwealth of Pennsylvania."[9] This case, which would have been rejected out of hand not too many years earlier, was concerned with the whole range of conditions that determine the quality of a prison operation.

The three Philadelphia prisons not only were subject to public neglect for years, but also were caught in the complex and grossly inefficient system of case processing which is all too typical of any metropolis. Jails stay full and prisoners wait interminably for trial because the defense, prosecutorial, and court services are impossibly overburdened.

In Philadelphia the prisons suffered from a glut of untried inmates as well as from almost all the ills to be found in ancient lockups everywhere. There was serious overcrowding, months of idleness for prisoners who wondered hopelessly when their cases would be heard, dungeonlike cells, leaky roofs, unsanitary food areas, insufficient staff, inadequate medical services, little recreation, and a severely decrepit physical plant.

[8] *Ibid.*
[9] Gerald Jackson v. Hendrick, in the Court of Common Pleas for the County of Philadelphia, Pennsylvania. Decided April 7, 1972.

After a protracted trial, the court found that the prison conditions did indeed constitute an invasion of constitutional rights as alleged. The court retained jurisdiction and ordered the appointment of a master to oversee prompt and explicit improvements.

In this case the court took an approach that should be appreciated by prison administrators who often view the usual adversary actions of the authorities as being little short of villainous. The Philadelphia court recognized that the problem is not so simple. "Finally, it is not to be thought that the Court is making findings of fault. Such a conclusion would represent a grave misunderstanding, both of the findings and of the Court's intention. The cause of the prisons' condition is too complex to permit findings of fault; and even if this were not the case, more often than not to find fault causes misunderstanding and bitterness."[10]

This statesmanlike approach is very fitting, for even in the cases brought by individual prisoners alleging gross and cruel misuse of segregation it is not a simple matter of all the right being on one side or the other. At such times the formal legal language of complaint and findings obscures the highly charged emotional situation from which the suit usually arises. The inmate is not just a passive victim of monstrous custodians, but is instead likely to be an articulate, aggressive, litigious, and provocative person who is superbly clever at exhausting the patience of the prison administrators and capitalizing on their errors. The militant inmate and the custodians are both caught in an untenable situation. The militant, perhaps revolutionary, inmate recognizes the gross unfairnesses of the whole criminal justice process, of which the prison is the most tangible and visible element, and he is driven by his own principles to exploit the captive prisoner audience around him.

It is true that the custodians, with or without any real understanding of the militant viewpoint, overreact in their use of punitive segregation, but they do so quite humanly. While some of the reaction may be spiteful, it must be said in fairness that the guards are also reacting genuinely out of their proper concern for the safety of a

[10] *Ibid.*

highly volatile institution. Their concern is legitimate; the overkill is not. By using prolonged segregation the prison asserts its control and keeps the prisoner from fomenting rebellion among the others — temporarily. But when the case comes to court the prison loses. It loses twice: once in court and once back among the cell blocks, for the prisoner is back with his captive audience again and this time is supported by more evidence of authoritative misdealings.

The prisoner is right when he shouts that the whole system is oppressive. But the custodians are also right that his shouts endanger security. Furthermore, wardens are resentful that their work is decried as denying the constitutional rights of prisoners when all they intended was to operate a properly controlled and secure institution.

It is an understandable feeling, but the way to a solution is not through the taking of unconstitutional liberties in even the most provocative cases. The militant prisoner must be granted all the privileges given to any other, even though it means setting the prison on top of a powder keg. In a perverse sort of way, such a dangerous condition will be a service to us. In long-term effect, the court cases will serve best, not in the relief of individual inmates as much as in forcing acceptance of the view that prisons are so basically inimical to the rights of human beings that improvement in their management will never be enough. Abolition in their present form will have to come.

CHAPTER 9

Toward a More Corrective Prison

PROBABLY NO concept has ever been so honored in the breach instead of in the observance than the splendid idea that offenders, if they must be imprisoned, should go to prison *as* punishment rather than *for* punishment.

If punishment is what society seeks to impose upon the offender, then simple loss of liberty is punishment enough. Even in these liberty-loving United States this fact is not fully appreciated. The public is constantly worrying that any physical or program improvements introduced into prisons will "coddle" prisoners and reduce the deterrent effect of what is supposed to be punishment. Such a thought should forever be dismissed. No amount of country club type comforts in a prison could possibly make it other than punishment when it still brings loss of liberty and loss of free socializing with family, friends, and the outside world. In terms of simple creature comforts some men do live better in some prisons than they do outside, but they are no less eager for release.

Once we are fully persuaded that loss of liberty punishes sufficiently and just as sufficiently protects the public from the imprisoned person, we should then be ready to abandon the conditions that heap extra humiliation and defeats upon the prisoner.

128

Then we will be ready to grant to him all the normal practices of a responsible person as far as these can be accomplished within the operation of a prison. A good example of such a practice is the opportunity to correspond freely, which has already been discussed. It cannot be said that prisons have restricted correspondence privileges to compound the punishment; the rationale has instead been that the restriction strengthens prison security. But there is no doubt whatever that the security argument has been heavily supported by the general feeling — even a virtuous sort of feeling — that prisoners do not really deserve the kinds of privileges that law-abiding people have.

Here penal reformers are confronted with the instinctive and emotional feelings of the public, and must deal perpetually with this altogether human resentment against money being spent to provide "advantages" to prisoners who, because of their adjudicated misbehavior, do not merit such advantages. But as a simple and practical argument, it is not so important what the inmate deserves as it is that we make him law abiding so that when he emerges from prison other citizens will be safe from him. And it is more likely that he will emerge with a good attitude if he has been treated with humaneness and decency. Conversely, if he is subjected to deprivation and extra disabilities on top of the loss of liberty, he may emerge with increased resentment toward society and will be a more dangerous person than before. Whenever this is so the punishment has completely defeated any useful purpose it was supposed to have.

A true application of this philosophy must mean the abolition of jails and prisons as they now exist; but while we still have them we can do a few things differently in them to help the inmates, or at least to reduce the harm they too often do. The following fifteen concepts cover some of the more obvious areas of needed improvement.

1. *No offender should be sent to prison for his own good. That is, no one should be committed to or retained in prison just for the sake of treatment or rehabilitation.*

This is not to suggest that prisons should be excused from the job of rehabilitation. Quite the contrary. The court, in committing a man to prison, may quite properly have in mind that the prison has the treatment or training programs that the defendant needs. However, the outside community also has such services, and more; so the defendant should never be in prison just for the sake of its helping services — but only when it seems imperative that first of all he needs to be in custody.

If this principle is taken seriously, it will no longer be valid for a parole board to extend a man's term because he needs to take further advantage of some institutional program. If it is that important for the inmate to have that kind of help, it is incumbent on the state to provide it in the community. If the service is to be given in the institution, it must be only if custody also is needed.

2. *Insofar as the realistic problems of prison security and order will permit, the prisoner is not to be thwarted in living the way he wants if he can pursue that life style without criminal activity.*

It is almost a universal aspect of correctional history that courts, correctional officials, parole boards, and probation or parole officers have used their authoritative control to require of the offender a conventional life style, complete with standard middle-class values. The present-day militance of various groups with particular cultural, ethnic, or racial interests is helping to reveal this condition and at the same time is leading to its reduction. As parole boards are confronted with inmates who very pointedly show loyalty to unconventional life styles or maverick political views, it has become more sharply evident that an inmate's unwillingness to conform to traditional middle-class values tends to delay his release even if he quite clearly is not dangerous.

This can be true even where the parole board considers itself unprejudiced in this regard, for the parole delay can result indirectly from the prisoner's previous occasional defiance of petty institutional rules, his subsequent punishment, and his bad conduct record which dampens his parole chances.

Admittedly this principle of allowing individual life styles will be more applicable in the parole setting than in prison where regimentation is unavoidable. But latitude is possible in certain areas, such as the right to individual styles in hair, dress, religion, reading materials, and cell decorations.

3. *Communication must be enhanced.*

The prisoner is in great need of keeping in touch with the outside community and this can be enhanced in a variety of ways. The liberalization of mail privileges is an obvious means and because of comments in previous chapters requires no further argument here except to say that the standard prison rule must be that, if a prisoner wants to pay the postage, he be allowed unlimited freedom to send out uncensored mail to any correspondents in any quantity, and that he be allowed to receive mail just as generously with no more inspection than is necessary for interception of contraband. (Actual experience with the lifting of mail restrictions shows that after an initial flurry of letter writing the volume of mail settles down to a steady level not much different from that under censorship restrictions.) In certain prisons at certain times it may be realistic and necessary to forbid entrance of materials which seem to incite and instruct rebellious activities.

Telephone privileges should also be greatly increased. The only apparent reason for denying telephone use to prisoners (other than wanting to avoid "coddling") would seem to be a fear of security risk or a budget problem. As long as a prisoner can talk face to face with a visitor, there can hardly be extra security risk in allowing conversations by telephone. The one problem remaining is the extra cost for extra phones and the staff effort needed to supervise and control the calling. Yet it is worth the cost and effort, and it usually would be feasible to work out a procedure for prisoners to pay for their calls.

4. *A system of furloughs should be set up to reward progress and to serve the essential purpose of keeping inmates oriented to family and community.*

The Scandinavian countries have pioneered in the use of furloughs and have demonstrated that this means of keeping a man in touch with his family can be quite workable. In Sweden, for instance, certain prisoners are eligible for their first furlough after four months in prison, and subsequent furloughs can be granted every three months. The first furlough is for forty-eight hours, plus travel time, and later the time may be increased to as much as seventy-two hours. The Swedish National Correctional Administration reports that in 1970 it granted 14,270 furloughs and all but 8.8 percent of these prisoners returned. Another 4 percent returned late or were guilty of violations such as drinking.

Although there has been little systematic use of furloughs in the United States, the practice has been quietly in use in one state where it might be least expected. Arkansas, even during the years when its prisons earned their unsavory reputation, had a well-designed furlough program in operation. Fortunately in the last few years the furlough idea has been gaining acceptance in many states.

5. *The convict should not escape civic responsibilities just because he is incarcerated. He should be permitted and expected to vote and to render occasional public service.*

The convict's loss of the right to vote is one of those issues mainly rooted in history, rather than being grounded in any practical and currently valid logic. Victor Hugo portrayed with deep feeling the predicament of convicts and ex-convicts in eighteenth-century France. Not only did Jean Valjean, the hero of *Les Miserables*, suffer the cruelties of French prison life and toil for many years, but upon release he was permanently crippled by a distinctive passport which revealed his ex-convict status wherever he went. It made him a nonperson whom the villagers turned their dogs upon even when he sought the simplest amenities of a meal and lodging. Hugo's story has the power to move us deeply and to make us feel smugly pleased that we are not like that today. Today we are much more subtle. We actually engage in many efforts to help the ex-convict regain his life in the community — but still with us is the heritage of punitive denial of civil responsibilities and rights.

Why is a convict not allowed to vote? The right to vote would not jeopardize the control and security of the prison. The reason lies mainly in the historical fact that our laws were written this way so long ago that they are simply taken for granted today. But if the question is actually faced, the usual defense would be that the right to vote is a privilege and the prisoner by his offense against the state has forfeited such privileges.

Today's rebuttal to this must be that the right to vote is also a responsibility and above all the process of rehabilitation is a process of teaching the offender to be responsible. Crime is a function of irresponsibility, and if we are to reverse a criminal career, we will do so only by helping the offender to become more responsible in every aspect of his life, including civic duties. A child learns to ride a bicycle only by riding a bicycle, not by going to bed. A person will not learn to exercise responsibility by being put in an institution where all responsibilities are denied him.

Of course it cannot be argued that by setting up voting booths in prisons we will measurably increase our rehabilitative effect. Rehabilitation is not just one kind of program but derives from many kinds of activities, efforts, and conditions in all areas of prison management, and all of these, including the right to vote, must be supported if the objective is fully to be gained.

Another treatment element to be offered must be the opportunity to serve. This is an aspect of the ordinary citizen's life that is vital for giving him a sense of pride and self-worth. Every civic club has its service projects. The opportunities to do volunteer or church work, to give blood, or to be a Cub Scout den mother are legion. Practically every citizen gets involved in serving his community even if it is nothing more than giving a dollar when the neighbor lady comes around to collect for the heart fund.

But again the prisoner is denied the healing and maturing quality of this kind of activity. There are occasional reports of a convict group adopting a project and getting publicity for contributing to some particular cause, but this ordinarily is an accidental development and not part of the regular prison program.

No other organization would operate in that way. A junior chamber of commerce chapter would not exist without a service project it could energetically pursue. The Alcoholics Anonymous organization knows that the indispensable ingredient in its treatment program is to keep each member busy helping other alcoholics. The day must come when any prison that pretends to make a rehabilitation effort will have regularly structured service projects which involve most inmates. To some extent, depending on local circumstances, these may in some way serve the outside community, and there would be some special advantages to this arrangement. But other projects may serve inside the prison by being self-help efforts, and some may be in the form of opportunities for individual inmates to help other inmates.

In any prison the inmates are assigned to jobs, some of which are services to the inmate population. Prisoners have their hair cut by other prisoners; a prisoner's laundry is done by prisoners; simple medical assistance is given by inmates employed in the prison hospital. Why not a counseling assignment? To an extremely limited extent it has been tried. In one courageous experiment in North Carolina, a small prison camp was operated with a staff of five men all of whom had learned a dynamic brand of group therapy as prisoners in California. Because they had shown both convincing personal progress and a skill in conducting or teaching the process they were hired to run a prison camp and its therapy program.[1]

There is no reason why convicts who show this degree of personal progress and skill cannot be used in this way while still in prison. It depends, of course, on the presence of a truly effective therapy program to develop the inmate counselors in the first place, but this program should be there anyway. Then when any inmate has progressed to the point of being able to help others, his regular job assignment could be in counseling. It has long since been discovered that this brings a therapeutic sense of mission and self-worth to the counselor, as well as a particularly effective help to his clients.

6. *Employment in prison should, as far as possible, be characteristic of employment outside.*

In its simplest terms this is a proposal to allow each inmate to apply in a formal manner for the prison job he wishes to have; to be hired for that job if an opening is available and if he is qualified; and to be paid full wages commensurate with the going rates in the outside community. It would then follow that he would also be

---

[1] Paul W. Keve, *Imaginative Programming in Probation and Parole* (Minneapolis: University of Minnesota Press, 1967), p. 212.

charged for the services and goods provided by the prison. He would pay rent on his cell, he would pay for his laundry and medical expenses, and he would pay admission to movies or other entertainment. A weekly meal ticket could be purchased, and in going through the cafeteria line each man would select whatever food items he wishes and his meal ticket would be punched accordingly. He could eat sparely or lavishly as he might wish.

The prison might well contain a branch bank and prisoners could maintain both checking and savings accounts. Even loans would be arranged under certain circumstances. Probably specie would be used for legal tender within the institution instead of real money.

Some of the value of this approach can best be appreciated by comparing it with the more conventional prison operation. Ordinarily a prisoner is assigned to a specific job in prison and if at any time he rebels against it he is subject to disciplinary measures for refusing to work. In the dining room he is allowed to take what he wants to eat but is usually subject to a rule that he must eat all he takes, or be subject to discipline. These are rules that have been taken for granted and regarded as virtues as long as there have been prisons. But these conditions unnecessarily reverse the social situation of the outside world. For the rest of us there is no law that says we must work. We are punished for offenses which may result from not working — nonsupport of family, nonpayment of debt, etc. — but if a person can meet his legal obligations without working he is under no legal requirement to go to a job every day. Similarly, though it is considered virtuous to avoid wasting food, there is no requirement in the outside world that a person must clean his plate. In prison we tend to forget what is normal and impose these rules to enforce what is not necessity but only virtue, and with every such rule we create a new group of rule breakers, keeping us busy punishing people for actions that are bad only in an artificial, institutional sense.

Much of this could be avoided by instituting a normal economic system in the prison. Let the prisoner obtain a job by applying and qualifying for it. If occasionally he is not in the mood to work let that lapse be treated as casually as if it were in the outside community.

The penalty would be the same that faces us outside. He would suffer only from the loss of wages and from the loss of such goods and services that the unearned money could have purchased. If his job absenteeism is excessive, he would additionally suffer the possibility of being fired. If his poor job management results in substantial economic failure, he could be evicted from his private cell and left to sleep on a cot in some open space (the equivalent of the park bench) without privacy.

In those cases where this kind of irresponsibility is persistent, extra counseling would be necessary to help the prisoner with this problem. It is here, while we have him in prison, that we should make the most of our opportunity to discover what problems he has in this regard and to give him realistic help with them.

The introduction of such a system will instinctively be resisted by many prison employees and administrators who will marshal a variety of arguments against it just as every prison improvement has been instinctively opposed since such institutions began. But the idea is beginning to be talked about and in fewer years than might be expected it will become commonplace. The most obvious impediment to it from the legislator's viewpoint will be that it will require an enormously increased prison budget. Legislatures now finance prisoner pay up to about a dollar a day in some of the more generous states; other states finance as little as five cents a day and some provide no wages at all. To move to full union-scale wages would be an enormous jump. But the jump will be made tolerable by the return of a substantial part of the wages paid. For instance, the inmate would be charged the full cost of his food, which the state now gives him free. In addition to paying cell rent and paying for various services, he would be required to send part of his pay to any dependents he has and this would offset welfare costs to that extent.

An obvious objection to the plan is that it simply will not work for some prisoners. This is true. Every prison has a few physically incapacitated men who cannot work, and there are always those who are so maladjusted that they are frequently in segregation or otherwise not available or not reliable enough for regular work. This is similar to life on the outside where a percentage of people must always be incapacitated for some reason, but still the world of work goes on for those who can and will work. In a prison it may be necessary for the full wage work program to be applied only to certain cell blocks or wings, with other parts of the prison reserved for the prisoners who cannot fit into this type of regimen.

One setting in which the full wage plan (the Swedish correctional system refers to it as the "market adapted wage") will be especially appropriate is the large urban jail which houses a substantial number of unconvicted prisoners awaiting trial. Usually it is assumed that such prisoners, being unconvicted, cannot be required to work, and this has sufficed as an excuse to provide little or no opportunity for them to work even if they want to. But there is no reason to refuse such a man the opportunity to work and support his family. He is not in jail either "as" or "for" punishment. He is there only to guarantee his presence at trial without new offenses in the interim.[2]

A possible answer to the work problem for this group would be to invite a private industry to set up and operate a shop within the jail. It would have to be some kind of assembly work that could be taught quickly and would not be too badly hurt by frequent turnover of workers. If this existed within the institution the unconvicted men could be hired by the entrepreneur operating the industry and could make full wages while awaiting trial. The family would continue to be supported and the terrible effects of prolonged idleness would be averted. There would be no "work relevance" issue as we constantly have with the license tag shops and some of the other typical prison jobs. If the work is in a production shop and pays full wages it is relevant.

It will not be easy to come up with the details of the successful

[2] On this general subject the New York State Special Commission on Attica (McKay Commission) took a forthright stand. Number 1 in its list of principles to serve as guidelines for restructuring of the prison system is the following: "If prisoners are to learn to bear the responsibilities of citizens, they must have all the rights of other citizens except those that have been specifically taken away by court order. In general, this means that prisoners should retain all rights except that of liberty of person. These include the right to be adequately compensated for work performed, the right to receive and send letters freely, the right to have and express political views, the right to practice a religion or to have none, and the right to be protected against summary punishment by state officials. When released from prison, they should not be saddled with legal disabilities which prevent them from exercising the rights of free men" (p. xvi).

operation of such an industry in a jail, but as long as any jail with a sizable population exists something of this kind is an important antidote to the degenerative character of jail life. Yet there is one answer that is better: no jail at all. It is proving quite realistic to develop pre-trial release programs that will retain safely in the community a high percentage of persons who now are jailed to await trial.

Another change needed to normalize prison employment is the discontinuance of "state use" laws. To appease both the manufacturers and the unions, we play this little game of pretending that competition with private industry is avoided by allowing prison industries to sell only to other governmental institutions and offices. It is an empty gesture. Every item sold to a government agency is one less item bought from private industry. If we eliminate the restrictive laws and allow prison industries to compete on the open market, it will not result in any more competition than there is now, and it will make possible more realistic employment for training prisoners. Outside industries have little to fear from a shop that can never increase its production beyond the level that can be sustained by a static prison population.

7. *Treatment services in prison must become more dynamic and realistic than anything commonly tried before.*

There is nothing incompatible between this idea and the principle that no one should be sent to or held in prison for his own good. In fact, the two concepts are mutually dependent and supportive. If a man is not required to accept any kind of training or treatment, if he will be released on a day certain whether or not he has availed himself of the treatment program, it then follows that the treatment offerings will have to be sufficiently real and vital to carry their own appeal.

A. The need for quality

A standard and well-entrenched view throughout the corrections field is that the clientele lacks motivation and consequently we are limited in what we can do for them. There is some truth to this idea but we have relied on it too much, and it has been an excuse for halfhearted effort. Consider instead the view of the authors of *Struggle for Justice*:

> There is a belief held by many, especially experts in the social service fields, that lower-class, emotionally disturbed, "deviant" or "criminal" persons most often are not aware of their real problems and will not seek services that can help them. We disagree totally with this proposition. In the first place, help must be defined from the viewpoint of the person in need, and in the second place, the reason a person in need turns his back on help is, by and large, that the services offered are shabby substitutes for help. When real services are available, those in need literally line up at the door.[3]

Echoing this opinion is a most interesting bit of personal testimony from an unlikely source. Eldridge Cleaver is, of course, a hostile revolutionary who deeply distrusts and despises prison custodians and sees the correctional system as repressive and phony. But there was one teacher at San Quentin whom he writes about with unabashed awe and respect. He tells of himself and other prisoners, by their own choice, sitting day after day in this particular class, accepting this teacher's exacting rules and giving him unwavering respect. Why? Essentially because this teacher was broadly knowledgeable, because he was talking with enthusiasm about the great ideas of great thinkers on social issues, and most essentially of all, because he had a simple, passionate, uncomplicated love of people and love of teaching. His presence at the prison every day seemed to have nothing to do with the fact of his having a job there. He was there because he was inwardly driven to give of himself. In other words, he was real.

This is the first and most fundamental clue to what a treatment program must be if it is to attract and hold a convict clientele without the help of any carrot held out by the parole board. And it presents us with a basic problem regarding the involvement of the guard staff: the problem is that the guard force likes to "have respect."

It would seem to be a logical and completely natural thing to expect inmates to be polite when accepting instructions from guards,

[3] The American Friends Service Committee, *Struggle for Justice*, p. 98.

but dynamic treatment programs have a way of reducing the façade of respectful demeanor that the guards like. The prison of the very near — the immediate — future cannot operate on the old rule that a guard must always be saluted and addressed respectfully as "sir" by the inmates. The guards today no longer expect the salute, but they do assume that they are entitled to certain courtesies that they think prisoners should show toward their custodians. They usually fail to realize that when a hostile, resentful, and consequently potentially dangerous inmate maintains a coerced demeanor of courtesy, he is only being deceptive rather than truly respectful.

Although this surface demeanor is satisfying to the guard, with more training he would learn that his own interests would be far better served if the prisoner's true feelings were not masked by feigned respect. It is when the inmate lets his feelings go and responds with bitter invective that the guard has the opportunity to perceive what the problem is and to institute measures to deal with it.

As a practical matter, guards should know just who is hostile, about what, and to what degree for the sake of their own safety. They should, for their own protection if for no other reason, not "demand respect" in a way that will mask the signs of danger. In fact, insisting upon outward signs of respect not only will serve to hide the potential danger points but will add to their intensity.

Does this mean that an inmate is to be allowed to insult and defy a guard at any time? Not really. It means that in a well-run prison opportunities must be scheduled for free-wheeling encounters between staff and inmates in situations where the talk can be entirely uninhibited.

For instance, it is not only possible, but therapeutic for a group of a dozen or so inmates and a staff member to have regular talk sessions that explore all their feelings and ideas. Such a meeting should be in a small room that ensures privacy, and it should be held at least weekly, and preferably daily. Perhaps two staff members may meet with the group and these can be members of the guard force. The session may be entirely free ranging, and as long as it is honest, it can and should include expression of any feelings, no matter how bitter, voiced in any language no matter how profane, obscene, or insulting. The rule should simply be that in this room among this group anyone can utter his honest feelings whatever they may be. The only restriction is that there be no physical violence and that no grudges be carried out of the room. This means that if an inmate has a gripe about a guard, even one of those in the room, he can express his gripe without restraint and the two can slug it out verbally without restraint. The inmate must have the assurance that whatever he says in the session is not to result in any reprisal, and the guard must be able to expect that in contacts outside that room the ordinary courtesies will again prevail. But in that room, issues of insubordination and the façade of respect simply do not exist. It is just a group of men looking for answers to a predicament that has impaled them all.[4]

B. The need for follow-through

This kind of group process has been used in a few adult correctional facilities, and some good research has been done to check its effectiveness in terms of recidivism. The results are disappointing. The rather too easily reached conclusion is that the process contributes to the stability of the institution, but it does not produce gains for the inmate that carry over reliably to outside living.[5]

This should not really be surprising. Here is a man who has many problems in adjusting to the competitive outside world; he is placed in a prison and taught — more or less — to live in that artificial society, and then he is released one day to live again in the world outside without much help in getting readjusted. We like to think that the purpose of parole is to give that assistance, but quite realistically a parole officer dividing his time among fifty or more

[4] For a detailed discussion of this technique as developed in the Highfields programs, see chapter 5 of Keve, *Imaginative Programming in Probation and Parole.*

Discussions of such programming in jails and other adult correctional facilities will be found in Norman Fenton, ed., *Explorations in the Use of Group Counseling in the County Correctional Program* (Palo Alto, Calif.: Pacific Books, 1962).

[5] As examples of research reports that show discouraging results of prison treatment programs see, James Robison and Gerald Smith, "The Effectiveness of Correctional Programs," *Crime and Delinquency,* vol. 17, no. 1 (January 1971), p. 67; Gene Kassebaum, David A. Ward, and Daniel M. Wilner, *Prison Treatment and Parole Survival: An Empirical Assessment* (New York: John Wiley, 1971).

cases does not help a newly released prisoner to the degree that help is needed.

In the institution the amount of staff time and the budget per inmate are excessive even without any elaborate treatment programs included. In the ordinary prison, it costs more to keep an inmate for a year than it would cost to send that man to Yale or Harvard for a year. But the amount we spend to keep our ex-prisoner stabilized during those crucial weeks after release is minuscule in comparison.

If we are to make the best possible use of the prison while we still have such places, we should persist in utilizing the most intensive treatment efforts, group therapy, or whatever else, but then the length of this expensive institutional stay should be substantially shortened and followed by a drastically increased amount of follow-through help in the community. Putting together the results of various research efforts and experimental programs, it becomes evident that the gains made in a prison treatment program probably can be retained if there is a follow-through service of exceptional intensity and quality. This means abandonment of any idea of getting by with the undifferentiated caseloads of forty to one hundred per worker which are typical now. Good caseload management suggests that it is acceptable for one parole officer to carry up to a hundred cases if these are low risk cases which do not require close supervision. But that approach is tolerable only if at the same time we use small caseloads for the higher risk cases and for most parolees during their first few weeks of adjustment to the outside world. For such a caseload a limit of ten may be realistic. (For more discussion of caseload management see pages 172–182.)

A caseload of ten or less may be objected to as absurdly expensive, but it would still be much cheaper than the institution, and with this close, daily kind of help a prisoner probably could be released earlier and the expensive extra time in prison could be avoided.

8. *We should at least experiment with the idea of a short, fixed length of stay as an alternative to the indeterminate sentence.*

After decades of espousing the indeterminate sentence and

release predicated upon good behavior, the corrections field is hearing new arguments that sentences should be for fixed terms with release guaranteed on a day certain. The validity of this is suggested by the experience with an intensive and dynamic group therapy process developed in New Jersey's Highfields programs. In that type of facility for older teenagers and young adults, the length of stay is ordinarily about four months and the group sessions are held at least five days a week. With this intensive effort, it is possible to impress upon the resident the fact that he has just four months to get in shape so that when he leaves, as he surely will after about that length of time, he will be able to stay out. The program is designed to give the residents no incentive for simulating improvement in order to impress a parole board. Instead, the residents are motivated entirely by daily facing of the fact that improvement must be made, and fast, if they are to avoid trouble in the future.

By reverting to the fixed sentence for adult prisoners, we will not suddenly have the answer to our problems. Dynamic improvements in the treatment program must be instituted in conjunction with the fixed sentence or else it will result in "dead time" — time spent waiting for release without being motivated to improve. But with the fixed sentence, we will have a more honest process in which we avoid all temptations to simulate improvement. It will make us provide treatment programs that are of high quality; and it will assure us that inmates who use them will do so from sincere motives because there will be no need to go through the motions in order to impress anybody.

Fixed and limited sentences followed by only six months of parole supervision should be tried for most prisoners with the exception of persistent and dangerous offenders. This would drastically reduce the demand upon parole board time, leaving it possible for the board to give proper attention to its other concerns. It would also improve parole service. The time when a new parolee needs help is during the first weeks following his release, and in most instances it is a waste of a parole officer's time to remain active with cases that are one to three years old. Terminating supervision of all cases after six months would be the most immediate and economical way of reducing a parole officer's caseload. As a concession to the reasonable fear that six months is too short as a time in many cases, an acceptable compromise would be to suspend active supervision at six months, keep the case in inactive parole status for another six months subject to being reactivated if necessary, and then finally close it out at the end of the twelve months if no new offenses have been reported.

9. *Academic and vocational education in prison needs a new vitality.*

Prisons have nearly always had educational programs, but they have tended to be anemic. In some institutions a prisoner may either accept part-time help from an inmate teacher or be given the opportunity to take correspondence courses. Prison teaching staffs are typically too small, poorly specialized, and poorly supplied with materials. Fortunately, the United States Office of Education (HEW), in cooperation with the Federal Bureau of Prisons, has in recent years taken a special interest in this condition of neglect and has supported an energetic effort to upgrade the quantity and quality of prison education. Under direction of faculty from the University of Hawaii, special training has been given to prison personnel throughout the country in the techniques of improved academic education in custodial situations.

Another development, financed by the Labor Department, is the Newgate program which is offering college-level education in several selected prisons. It goes far beyond the correspondence courses in providing an actual full-time, fully accredited college program for qualified prisoner students. Furthermore, there is provision for some scholarship help for students who are eventually paroled and want to attend outside university campuses as regular students.

The idea is not popular with some guards who grumble that their own children have no such help in getting through college and that it is grossly unfair to spend money to give such advantages to convicts. But we are already paying enormous sums to keep prisoners in our institutions, and the additional cost of some college tuition

is little enough to pay if it will enable a prisoner to increase his
chances of leading a law-abiding life.

A. Vocational training

No one seems to dispute the immense appropriateness of vocational training programs for prison inmates, and, in fact, it is commonplace for prisons to offer one or another kind of trade training.
Nevertheless, there still is great need for improvement since the
training programs generally are handicapped by the problem of
having to be relevant to the outside job market. Often they are
authorized by rather specifically worded statutes and cannot be
quickly changed to accommodate new trends in industry. Outmoded equipment cannot be replaced until the legislature appropriates the needed funds, and this is likely to be long after the
equipment is obsolete by outside industrial standards.

All of this serves to make the training program unimpressive to
the inmates and to reduce their motivation to learn. Vocational
instructors face daily the problem of the credibility gap with prisoners who either do not feel that the training actually will help them
with outside job prospects or else they develop unrealistic ideas of
the level of job or salary they will be able to get.

To meet all these demands more effectively, the prison must
cooperate far more with outside industry. As a possible first step,
the prison may make available to a local and major outside industry
some suitable shop space inside the prison complex. That industrial
company would then be responsible for setting up an operation that
may be a combination of training and actual production. In addition
to supervising the production job, it would be their function to·train
inmates in work that may lead to jobs in the company after release.

The possibility of such an enterprise being self-supporting for
the entrepreneur is still subject to experiment, but it will be well
worth it to the state to subsidize such programs to the extent of
providing free housing and utilities, including the power supply.

Under this arrangement, the work and training program would
realistically relate to the outside job world, and inmates would have
the great advantage of being able to talk with industrial representa-

tives who can give them a practical reflection of job prospects. Another important advantage would be the flexibility, for the shops operated by outside industries would be expected to change equipment or product lines needed to keep pace with real industrial demand.

10. *"Treatment services" should be a function of the custodial staff.*

This is another reversal of a favored notion, for it has been the almost universal practice for professional persons (caseworkers, sociologists, psychologists, teachers, etc.) to be hired and used quite separately from the custodial staff. The effect has been to make the custodial officers feel inferior because of the obvious differences in education, salary, and status between them and the treatment staff, and so the two have become competitive instead of cooperative. Since the custody people are more numerous and since it is they who have the keys, they usually gain final control even of the prison programs.

One outcome of this is that the inmates in most prisons usually hold the counseling staff in low esteem. Chaplains and caseworkers, for instance, are not highly regarded because, although they purport to be the "helping persons," they are not so in fact, owing largely to their lack of power. On this score, the custodial staff would be rated higher by the inmates except that often the guards' lack of training and their insensitivity offset the natural advantage they have.[6]

Instead of fighting the power of the custodial staff, it makes much better sense for corrections officers to utilize and enhance it. This would mean developing a career ladder within the personnel system, encouraging and to some extent subsidizing college studies for the guard force. Tied to the prescribed college curriculum would

[6] See Daniel Glaser, *The Effectiveness of a Prison and Parole System* (Indianapolis: Bobbs-Merrill, 1964), chapter 6.

In extensive querying of inmates in many institutions, Glaser found that work supervisors are most often the best-liked staff persons, while caseworkers seem to have so little impact on the inmates that they are not often mentioned as either liked or disliked. When a feeling about caseworkers was expressed at all, however, it was more often a feeling of dislike.

be potential opportunities for promotions and salary increases. Promotion to the lieutenant level should require completion of at least two years of college including some prescribed number of credits in courses appropriate to correctional work.

At the same time, certain custodial jobs should be defined as having counseling responsibilities in addition to conventional custodial duties. The lieutenant positions especially would be shaped in this direction as fast as qualified personnel could be developed. Guards should be encouraged, under qualified supervisory or consultative help, to carry voluntarily some group counseling activities, and good performance in this should count appreciably in qualifying for promotion. Where professionally trained casework staff now exist, as they do in many prisons, they should cease to carry direct casework responsibility and instead serve as trainers and consultants for the custodial staff members who undertake the counseling functions.

A natural question this raises is related to the great volume of desk work customarily handled by casework staff who must prepare classification summaries, case histories for the parole board, etc. How can the custodial staff take over the real burden of the paper work? The answer has to be found partly in a courageous determination to produce less paper. The professional time now spent in reading case material costs the taxpayers prodigious sums and has little helpful impact on the inmates. In most prisons a systematic appraisal must be made of those standard items of information that have true value in deciding a case, and then the accumulation and processing of information must be limited to those items. Much of the paper now going into case files should not be saved at all, and some of it should not be produced in the first place. This is particularly true of disciplinary reports on violations of prison rules. The parole board is likely to protest the unavailability of this material, but it is not just a matter of their being able to get along without it; in most cases they simply should not have it. Their job is to determine a man's readiness to live in the outside world, and a major defect in parole board functioning is the tendency to judge potential adjustment to *outside* living by the misleading quality of adjustment to *inside* living.

Another answer to the paper work problem is the emergence of the electronic handling of case information. The technology is now available to permit a drastic reduction in paper usage through electronic equipment with little appreciable increase in operational cost in most cases.

Altogether, the shifting of counseling responsibility to the custodial staff can make this service more real and available to the prisoners, and it can serve as a morale boost to the custodial staff by giving them a greater sense of worth, more opportunities for promotion, and a basis for improved salaries. And anything that improves custodial staff morale is of inestimable value as a basis for a smoother running institution in which there may be more constructive effect upon inmates.

11. *The staff must be trained.*

In many states the prison staffs now receive so little training that they need to start virtually from the beginning and build training programs more thorough and penetrating than anything commonly attempted thus far. The immense problem we face is that much of the training to be done is in the subtle areas of attitudes and ways of relating to prisoners. It is relatively easy to teach the more objective subjects like security measures and use of riot equipment, but it is very hard indeed to implant understanding and the compassion for people which will make the riot measures much less needed.

The difficulty of accomplishing this kind of improvement in staff functioning is seldom fully appreciated. In one state, a citizen's group had been studying the problems of a prison and then confronted the administration about improvements they considered imperative. Not surprisingly, they heard in return about some of the budget realities that are related to prison problems. One committee member, however, concerned very properly with the way that staff treats prisoners, insisted with great intensity and obviously with no fear of contradiction, "It doesn't cost anything to treat people with simple dignity and courtesy!"

The trouble with that statement is that it seems irrefutable if regarded uncritically, but in its practical application in the prison setting it just might not prove to be so true as it sounds. In the prison situation, the potential for irritation is exaggerated at the same time that capacity for understanding the feelings of one's protagonist seems to be blunted, and so a special sensitivity is called for if real courtesy is going to be accomplished. If a guard is not aware of the feelings of inmates, or of his own effect on them, then some fairly expensive training is needed, and we find that it does in fact cost a considerable amount of money to achieve simple courtesy. A substantial element of the cost is in the salaries needed for staff to take the place of those who are in training sessions. In a prison, where nearly every guard is on a post that has to be covered, it is not possible to pull men off the job to attend meetings of any kind unless the budget can tolerate the hiring of substitutes to replace them.

Training is not just a matter of instruction or the transmittal of information. Equally important is a continuing reciprocal sharing of experience, attitudes, and practice which allows for a consistent philosophy and a fairness in applying rules.

A down-to-earth example of the problem involved came from a group of inmates discussing their own problem of getting along with guards who apply rules inconsistently. They were in a prison with typical cells, each equipped with a toilet which had no seat or cover. Also typically, they liked to remedy this standard prison omission by contriving their own toilet covers. So a plywood board cut in the appropriate shape would serve to improve the appearance and also make a seat. The particular episode mentioned by this inmate group arose when one inmate painted his plywood toilet cover while the inmate in the adjoining cell, not having access to any paint, completely wrapped his cover in decorative tape. During a routine cell inspection the guard confiscated the taped toilet cover but not the painted one; the owner of the latter told this story.

This guy who lived next to me was hot as hell because the damn guard had taken his toilet seat, and he says to me, "I suppose he picked up yours too." I told him that mine hadn't been taken and then he was really mad and said he guessed it must have been because he was black. You see, the guard didn't bother to explain to him that paint is all right, but with that tape on there it might be possible to hide some contraband like money or drugs or something under the tape. If he had only explained this it wouldn't have been so bad.

If anyone thinks that the incident is too picayune and too utterly ordinary to be worth mentioning as an example of prison management problems, let him remember that prison problems are not wide-screen, cast-of-thousands sorts of things except in occasional rare episodes. Even big eruptions are compounded accumulations of minute irritations that in the aggregate have become intolerable because a man in prison cannot walk away from an irritation but has to live with it every day. If something like the incident of the toilet seat cover is multiplied by a hundred other minute irritations, a chronic and pervasive mood of anger will evolve from which riots erupt when the right spark occurs.

It was this same, but even more gross insensitivity on the part of the guards which helped to spark the previously mentioned riot in the Kansas Penitentiary. There had been a routine but thorough shakedown of all cells in the affected cell block the day before. The shakedown itself is something that inmates can ordinarily tolerate as one of the unavoidable inconveniences of prison life. But in this instance there was sharp resentment because guards were heavy-handed in their search, turning everything inside out and then leaving the cells in complete disarray without any respect for the order of the cells or the condition of the inmates' possessions.

Both these incidents illustrate that prison disturbances have their roots in actions that do not arise necessarily from meanness, but only from entirely natural insensitivity. There is no reason to expect that the ordinary man from the free world can come to work in a prison and bring with him an exquisite sensitivity to the special psychological factors which affect his relationships with the prisoners who live in this distorted environment. But there should be every reason to expect that all officers should get both the initial and the continuing training that will promote this sensitivity. This is the true shape of professionalism.

The fact that training for prison custodial officers is so meager in United States institutions is largely a result of the country's being divided into fifty states. By contrast, England's correctional institutions are all under the direction of the Home Office and with this single organization it is possible to maintain a strong central training service. The Wakefield Staff College is just across the street from Wakefield Prison which is used as needed for training experience. Any new prison officer, known as a POUT (Prison Officer under Training), receives two months of training at the Staff College before being assigned to one of about 120 different institutions throughout England.

With this many institutions to serve, there is always enough staff turnover to justify a continuing training program, but in the United States, with all its separate state administrations, we completely lose this important advantage. A corrections department that typically has no more than a dozen institutions, instead of England's 120, and sometimes has as few as three or four, cannot possibly justify an adequate training course for the few new employees it hires each year. The result has been that in many prisons a new guard is on the job after one day of orientation, and even though most prisons are now offering one to two weeks of training for each new officer, this is still seriously inadequate.

The United States has a potential solution to this within its Federal Bureau of Prisons. There are conflicting views of the role of the federal prison system, but what it could indeed do to extend its usefulness would be to offer its institutions as training centers for state correctional agencies. The states would not be compelled to use them, but if the federal government would offer an excellent training service without cost to the states, it would not be long before it would be thoroughly used.

At the same time, the federal institutions could serve states in another way. Some of the smaller states, with only one security institution each, have difficulty in protecting endangered prisoners or otherwise meeting the needs of a few inmates with special problems. The federal institutions could be administered not to duplicate state services, as they do now, but to supplement and augment state services by accepting individual state prisoners according to unusual needs such as protection, special medical care, or special training or rehabilitation.

12. *It is time for the ombudsman.*

The ombudsman has been tried very little in this country, and where it has been attempted there is uncertainty and an experimental flavor to it, but the need for an ombudsman in the prison is crucial.

In his most essential character, [the ombudsman is an independent agent who has free run of the prison, allowing any inmate to have easy and confidential access to him regarding any complaint or worry he may have.] Largely because of his mobility, independence, cultivated acquaintance with the sources of power, and his own personal persuasiveness, the ombudsman becomes an advocate for the prison population generally, or a "fixer" for specific individual inmate problems. He can get answers to questions; he can find outside resources to help an inmate who is unable to enlist such needed help himself; he can be a reciprocal interpreter between inmates, administrators, legislators, and the public; and he can be a good listener. The most difficult aspect of the arrangement is the question of his sponsorship. If he is an employee of the corrections department, his highly important credibility in the eyes of the inmates may be suspect, and his freedom of voice and action may be restricted. But if he is the employee of some other agency, the corrections administrators may be apprehensive about who he is and may impede the usefulness of the program. The issue of sponsorship is also significant for the sake of the "clout" the ombudsman needs to have. When he sets out to investigate a matter or to pursue solutions to a problem, he must have entree to records, offices, and official ears without obstruction. With all these concerns in mind, it will be found that in many states the ombudsman is on the staff of the governor, and in other states it will work best for him to be on the staff of an independent outside agency.

The position is needed because the inmates are showing increasing impatience with their powerlessness to combat official apathy and unfairness, real or apparent. Ever present among the complex causes of prison disturbances is most certainly this boiling-point frustration with official unconcern about problems that are crucial to the inmate but boring to the custodians. An ombudsman may not be able to find any magic solutions to the problems, but if nothing else, he can reduce tensions by being an honest listener who has complete freedom to seek solutions if such there are.

A useful current example is the experience in Minnesota where an ombudsman was appointed in July 1972. To avoid subservience to the corrections administration and to gain greater credibility with all concerned, the office was made an independent agency, authorized by the legislature and with the ombudsman appointed by the governor. The Minnesota Department of Corrections includes eight institutions, both adult and juvenile, and the ombudsman and his staff (seven persons by the second year) serve all these facilities.

The experience has shown the great importance of starting the program with a patient, tolerant, adaptive, low-key approach that will encourage the ombudsman's credibility in the view of both inmates and staff. An interesting feature of the Minnesota ombudsman is that he is available to consider complaints from staff as well as from inmates, although far more of the complaints come from inmates. Complaints are accepted whatever the source or the means of transmission, so the act of seeking help is not discouraged by any exacting or time-consuming application processes.

A prison administrator may easily fear that the ombudsman will circumvent or confuse some of the processes that the prison itself tries to maintain for dealing with the prisoner's problems, and of course an ombudsman who adopts a constantly adversary or competitive position in relation to the prison can cause this kind of antagonism. However, the Minnesota experience shows the possibility of a healthy opposite effect. The ombudsman's approach was to encourage inmates with complaints to utilize existing avenues of help within the institution, and this sometimes showed the inadequacy of these institutional resources. With further assistance from the ombudsman the administrators were in such cases able to sharpen the fairness and effectiveness of their processes and resources, which resulted in better solutions for the inmates without the inappropriate and divisive use of the ombudsman that would otherwise develop.

The range of problems accepted for attention by the Minnesota ombudsman office has been unlimited so far. In the first year of operation one prison experienced a disturbance in which an officer was held hostage by three prisoners. The ombudsman intervened at the invitation of all concerned and accomplished the release of the hostage and conclusion of the episode with no injuries to anyone. This not only was a substantial service but it also helped to enhance the new ombudsman's visibility and acceptance by both staff and inmates. His day-to-day services deal with individual complaints (a resented disciplinary action; an allegation of racial bias in some action taken against an inmate; a protested confinement in isolation) as well as policy and procedural matters (rules that are objected to for being unclear or unfair; inaccessible treatment or training programs; parole board practices). He provides a listening ear that gives inmates a needed sense of useful communication. He is able to give to administrators and staff a more sensitive awareness of the obtuseness of some of their procedures or conduct which they had comfortably regarded as being first rate. And the ombudsman has also proven to be useful, through his highly knowledgeable independence, in persuading the legislature to support certain needed appropriations or legislation.

13. *The inmate council can be useful.*

In a discussion of inmate councils at the 1972 Congress of Corrections, the executive secretary of the American Correctional Association was quoted as denigrating this concept, remarking that, "I can't see surrender of an institution to inmates any more than I can see surrender of the operation of an ocean liner to its passengers."[7]

The comparison is an appealing one, but defective. In the first place, the inmate council need not be designed to assume actual responsibility for prison operation, and, in fact, any "surrender" of administrative responsibility to the inmates would be contrary to everyone's interest. In the second place, the personal activities of passengers on an ocean liner are not subjected to minute-by-minute control, but are free from any interference by the captain. So the passengers do not need to protect their interests by having a say

[7] *Life* Magazine, September 8, 1972, p. 33.

in the ship's operation. Even if the situation were an oppressive one for the passengers, they would have to endure it for only a few days, and they would have numerous opportunities for relief.

But in prison the inmates are vitally affected by poor management, and they need experience in the democratic exercise of responsibility. If they are not given a legitimate chance to voice their concerns and to work to improve their condition, they will reach periodic boiling points when they "participate" in management destructively. Consequently, there seems to be strong argument for the use of inmate councils even though there have been countless sour experiences with them.

Most prison administrators are quick to assert that they do not want inmate councils because it has been shown repeatedly that they do not work. The only trouble with this view is that the utility of something is not disproved by experiences of failure that may be the result of defective design or leadership. Altogether, it seems safe to make the following points about the inmate council idea: (a) inmate councils can help inmates by giving them some practice in carrying responsibility; (b) they can be useful to the administration by reflecting the issues that are generating any abnormal temperature in the prison, thus contributing to its safe operation; (c) they should be given the fullest opportunity to exercise real and explicitly defined responsibility, subject to the clear right of the administration to retain final authority; (d) in exercising its right of veto over council decisions or recommendations, the administration must give honest and unambiguous reasons for the veto; (e) within the limits of well-understood and honestly sustained rules, the council members should be given latitude to determine their own style of operation; (f) and finally, it seems quite evident that the real key to the success of the inmate council is the administration's capability to provide leadership for this kind of thing. This last point is probably the most important one. The management of a prison is more an art than a science, and if any warden truly does not believe in the inmate council and would be uncomfortable working with one, it is probably well for him not to try it. Whatever the other conditions required for the success of a council, it will fail if the administrative leadership is not skillful, determined, and quite convinced of the worth of the idea.

14. *Conjugal visits? Well, maybe.*

The idea of allowing conjugal visits to prisoners is rapidly gaining ground in a general social climate that is getting more relaxed and permissive in sexual matters. At this time there is widespread feeling that prisoners should indeed be allowed some sexual contact, at least with their wives; and it is increasingly probable that conjugal visits will meet with public acceptance in the early future.

This does not mean that we are becoming truly rational in our approach to the issue, however. Where the idea is promoted, it is thought of only for male prisoners, for instance. It is rarely mentioned as something to which female prisoners should be entitled. In Mississippi, conjugal visits have been permitted for several decades, but for a long time they were allowed only to black prisoners, since they were less subject to moral strictures in the Southern culture. Eventually Mississippi granted the privilege to white prisoners also, and finally, in 1972, extended it for the first time to female prisoners.

It would seem quite consistent with the general theme of this book to advocate regular opportunities for normal sexual activity for all prisoners. For instance, it would be a useful privilege to use for motivating prisoners to behave better; it would help keep some important relationships alive and vital; it would help to reduce illicit and exploitive sex practices. But with a thoughtful look at that word *normal*, it seems best to suggest caution about the idea of the conjugal visit. The Mississippi experience reveals what anyone might expect: that even in some intact marriages the couple prefer not to use their visiting time for sexual activity. Sexual intercourse is far more than a quick physical act, and it is very private. In a large prison, the logistics of processing a substantial volume of such visits would likely result in an assembly-line routine without the needed real quality of privacy and dignity.[8]

[8] For an extensive discussion of the Mississippi experience, see Columbus B. Hopper, *Sex in Prison: The Mississippi Experiment with Conjugal Visiting* (Baton Rouge: Louisiana State University Press, 1969).

The typical prison with its barred cells simply could not accommodate the practice without somehow acquiring a row of enclosed rooms which would be scheduled on visiting days for a succession of half-hour liaisons which would be much too public despite a briefly closed door. The Mississippi experience also points up the problem of the prisoner without an intact marriage. This includes a heavy percentage of prisoners, and a conjugal visit policy offers them nothing but the possibility of becoming still more resentful.

There are certain other avenues for meeting the sexual need at least partially. For prisoners who are approaching release dates, there is now some opportunity for weekend family visits. A prison that has some unused staff quarters can make these available for a prisoner's family to come and spend a couple of days. Rather than being just a quick sexual liaison, such visits would be a whole family reunion, incidentally allowing husband and wife to sleep together for a couple of nights. It has the disadvantage of being possible only for a few prisoners, and only for the latter weeks or months of a prison term. The California institutions have developed this family visiting extensively and have studied the results systematically. "The central finding of this research is the discovery of a strong and consistently positive relationship between parole success and the maintenance of strong family ties while in prison."[9]

A second possibility is found in those few prisons which house their inmates in enclosed single rooms. With solid-wall rooms and liberal visiting arrangements, a prisoner could be allowed to talk with his visitor whenever he wished in his own room. There need be no mention of conjugal visits, just visits. If he may talk with his visitor in his own room with the door closed it is of no one else's concern what more they do as long as it does not endanger others. This would be the most satisfactory solution of all in respect to the needs of the majority of prisoners. The obvious drawback is that most prisons are not built this way and cannot feasibly be remodeled.

[9] Norman Holt and Donald Miller, *Explorations in Inmate-Family Relationships*, report number 46, Research Division, Department of Corrections, State of California, January 1972, p. 61.

A third approach is the furlough, which has already been discussed. Furloughs offer the most normal kind of opportunity for those who qualify for them. Of course it is no answer at all for those who do not qualify.

Since the presence of abnormal and predatory sex practices is one of the arguments favoring the introduction of conjugal visits, the point should be made here that there are other ways of reducing the gross sexual abuses that are endemic in some prison populations. A prison without conjugal visits can, nevertheless, operate with a minimum of vicious sexual abuses if it meets the other demands of humane care. Sex degeneracy in prison is an utterly natural concomitance of enforced idleness, not enough healthy and constructive stimulation, persistent boredom, and lack of adequate staff. Conversely, the prison can keep the problem within tolerable and nondestructive limits if there is meaningful work for everyone, varied and daily recreational activities, single occupancy cells, inmate wages, and adequate and considerate staff supervision.

Altogether, in this issue too, we must recognize that there just is no satisfactory answer. The best solutions we can find will satisfy the needs of only a small proportion of the prison population, and only occasionally. Conditions inherent in prison operation will frustrate us in this respect as long as we persist in maintaining such institutions.

15. *The segregation unit needs intensive service.*

The prisoners call it "the hole"; the administration may call it segregation, isolation, or "the adjustment unit"; but whatever the name, every prison has to have some place to segregate from the general prison population those inmates who are so overtly hostile that they jeopardize institutional security. In fact, if we accomplish real success in the overall improvement of correctional programs, one sign of progress may be that an increasing proportion of prison inmates will need segregation, for ideally those who are more amenable will be dealt with in the intensive noninstitutional programs, and the future prison will mainly house just the more seriously disturbed clientele. This effect is already being noted in many prisons.

The segregation unit in almost every prison is a problem that seems to have no satisfactory answer. These units have invariably been built to provide residence only, without provision for any type of program activity. They usually consist of a separate cell block with perhaps a small adjacent yard for occasional outdoor exercise, though the yards seldom are large enough for anything more than a short walk.

This situation is tolerable for the inmate who is housed there very briefly, and, of course, that is the thought behind the design of the area. The lack of activity during a week or so of punitive segregation does not necessarily have any deleterious effect upon a prisoner. But a prison of any appreciable size is always certain to have a few inmates who are utterly incapable of living elsewhere in the prison. They typically start fights without apparent provocation, with either staff or inmates, and impulsively use anything at hand for a weapon. Such an inmate needs very special handling, not for just a week of punishment, but for a prolonged period of time.

But to be constantly alone in a cell without social contacts and productive activity is more than the human psyche can tolerate without damage. The warden is usually faced with a dilemma — either to protect the prison security at the cost of keeping the prisoner in a segregation unit cell for months, perhaps years, or to return the prisoner to the regular cell block and program for the sake of his sanity, but at the risk of almost certain new trouble.

Actually, for most of these special problem prisoners, it is the prison life itself with its constant confinement and ever-present controls that provokes them, making them more dangerous than they would be if free in the outside world. In such cases the even tighter and more restricted climate of segregation exacerbates the problem, causes additional hostile reactions, and so defeats its purpose. For these prisoners a better answer could be a job on the big farm type of prisons which have had such unsavory reputations, but which offer the opportunity to put a prisoner on a remote job on the open farm where there is little or no contact with others. However, even if selection of these cases could be reliably made, the average prison has no such work placement to offer, and so while the prison exists, a way must be found to deal with the disturbed inmate in long-term segregation.

One of the more notable efforts in this direction was launched in 1971 in the Illinois State Penitentiary (Stateville). The plan was to establish a rich program of individual and group counseling, varied recreational activities, educational opportunities, work assignments, and religious guidance for men who were chronically in trouble in the general prison population.

To provide incentive, a three-stage progression through different levels of privileges had to be accomplished before the prisoner could return to the general population. Unlike the usual segregation where lack of activity necessitates that the length of stay be short, this segregation program was designed to provide much more activity, much less cell time, and consequently could serve any one prisoner over a longer period of time. It was the policy that an inmate's case would be reviewed every thirty days for possible progress to the next level. An inmate not only could be moved ahead to levels of more privilege, but also could be demoted if his behavior were unsatisfactory.

To make such a program work, it must, of course, be heavily staffed. In this instance the budget called for enough custodial staff so that there was about one officer to every two inmates, an especially rich ratio. In addition, there were funds for a treatment staff with clinicians from psychiatry, psychology, and medicine and for specialists in sociology, counseling, and recreation.

The plan got off to a shaky start in August 1971 and came to a halt ten months later, for reasons which in themselves are revealing of very real prison management problems as well as the legal considerations that must be reckoned with.

Some difficulty was encountered in getting all the treatment staff positions filled, and the traditional housing that had to be used was a built-in impediment. No matter how brilliant the program concept, the locale was still an old prison cell block with terribly limited space for out-of-cell activities and no private space at all for counseling. Also, the physical arrangement did not permit any productive work programs to be introduced so the work was mostly limited to the usual housekeeping jobs plus some assistance with other programs; library work, for instance. But finally, it was not these problems but court action which stopped the program.

Shortly before the opening of the Special Program Unit (SPU), the institution had experienced a general disturbance which was precipitated by an incident on the ball field. There followed a general lockup of the population, and then as prisoners were gradually unlocked, certain ones, presumed to be the provocateurs, were retained in lockup and transferred to the new segregation unit which was just then, quite coincidentally, getting started.

The American Civil Liberties Union had already brought legal action against the penitentiary for keeping men in punitive lockup without formal charges and hearings, so the new SPU started its existence under the shadow of legal protest in federal court. The class action suit charged that the assignment of prisoners to the SPU was, in effect, punishment and was accomplished without due process; it also charged that conditions in the SPU constituted cruel and unusual punishment.

The court gave the penitentiary credit for its efforts to give constructive help but agreed with the ACLU that the SPU was actually a form of punishment and so any inmate placed in it should first have an administrative hearing to satisfy the concept of due process. This hearing would include informing the inmate of the accusations against him and giving him opportunity to respond. The ACLU allegation of cruel and unusual punishment was rejected.

The effect of the decision was that all inmates were released from the SPU unless their continuance in it could be justified in an administrative hearing; thereafter the program could not be used for inmates who appeared to need this special help but could not be charged with a specific punishable act. It meant that the SPU as it was had to be halted and that the staff had to start over to find a new approach.

If the program had operated longer, it could have helped to answer a most perplexing question: Can a program in which an inmate must earn his way out really deal with the most seriously hostile prisoner? The offering of incentives for progress and the provision of demotion for recurring rebellious acts are supposedly sound clinical procedures. But it has a reverse effect on certain prisoners. Some men are so hostile and so willing to hurt themselves along with their custodians that they will use the system to defeat the system. For instance, by telling a man that he cannot get out of segregation unless he meets certain good behavior standards, we give him the opportunity to embarrass us with our own rules. By refusing to play our game, he keeps himself at the bottom level of segregation month after month until the custodians must in effect admit the failure of their program by finding some other way to get him out.

Danish psychiatrist and prison administrator Georg K. Sturup cautions against any approach which in essence says to the prisoner, "You are here because you need to be helped." That gives the prisoner the chance to defy us by continuing to be bad and thus proving that our help is ineffective — and consequently unneeded. Instead, Dr. Sturup says to his prisoners that "you are here in order for society to be protected against you."

This approach is at least a more honest one, and it means that the only way a defiant prisoner can prove us wrong is to behave nonoffensively in order to show that we were wrong in presuming that anyone needed to be protected from him. It is not quite so simple as that, of course, but it may give a clue to the problem of segregation in all our prisons. Every warden has known some prisoners who have stayed in isolated lockup for years. It is this kind of human waste and tragedy that the Illinois SPU is attempting to prevent. It will not prevent it in every instance, but every effort like this must be encouraged in order to reduce the number of men who defeat the system by means of their own personal defeat.

Whatever we do for the self-destructive prisoner, we will always find that the concept and structure of the program is not nearly so vital as the staff's skill, charisma, and quality of concern. In the final analysis, the effectiveness of treatment does not come from program design but from people who care. And that is at the same time our frustration and our hope.

What Will It All Accomplish?

A diligent application of the foregoing measures will make our prisons less destructive in their effect and will represent the least that a civilized nation should do. But these improvements will not stop escapes, they will not prevent riots, nor will they, by themselves, appreciably reduce recidivism rates.[10]

This seems a discouraging prospect, but it must be honestly faced. Any time that a substantial improvement is made in how a prison treats its inmates, there is an immediate modest improvement in morale and even something akin to gratitude on the part of the men or women confined. But in a few weeks, a few months, more and more new prisoners are present who did not know how it was before, and the improved conditions make no impression on them. The prisoners who do remember slowly lose their awareness of the change and turn their concern to the continuing daily struggle in the prison environment where life remains grim no matter how many amenities are introduced around the edges. In fact, the alleviation of prison miseries may have the effect of stimulating prison unrest. This is only for the same reason that we are contending with social unrest in the streets and ghettos throughout the world. People who are born into a life with no hope, no expectations, and no evidence of upward mobility for their kind are those most likely to be passive and to suffer their lot without serious protest. But when they begin to taste more privileged living and to believe themselves entitled to opportunity, then they begin to reach for power — destructively, if that is the only way possible.

It is happening elsewhere in our society; there is no reason to expect the prison world to escape from it. Indeed, the massive prison, which cannot be operated without imposing indignities upon its inmates, will increasingly be the crucible where this social struggle will be seen in its most anguished condition.

[10] "If the criminal justice system fails to dispense justice and impose punishment fairly, equally, and swiftly, there can be little hope of rehabilitating the offender after he is processed through that system and deposited in a prison — even a prison remodeled on the principles enunciated above." From *Attica*, the official report of the New York State Commission on Attica (New York: Bantam Books, 1972), p. xix.

So the message in this chapter is not that by instituting these improvements we can go on operating safe and useful prisons for a few more decades. Quite the contrary. The prison, even at its best, is inherently inimical to the human spirit, and all these improvements will help to make prisoners still more discontent with limited gains; will give them new aspirations for self-assertion and for the defeat of the institution. We are caught in a juggernaut of social change. While we have our prisons, we must improve them; first, simply because it is right to do so, and second, because court actions and prisoner actions are going to force change anyway.

But change begets change, and at an accelerating rate it will become apparent that — again, except for the dangerous few — the improved prison will make still more clear its inability either to reform its residents or to protect the rest of us.

CHAPTER 10

Instead of Prison

ANY SUBSTANTIAL move away from the use of prisons will be accomplished only if even more substantial moves are made to develop alternative programs. Nor is that all. Extensive readjustments must be made in our general philosophy of punishment and deterrence, and in our sentencing practices. Unthinking acceptance of the indeterminate sentence will have to yield, and this is asking a great deal of a public that has for so long taken for granted the virtue of this sentencing approach.

A delegate to an early American Prison Association meeting referred to "the indeterminate sentence, which despite the attacks made upon it, is doubtless the greatest contribution made by constructive penology toward the treatment of the offender."[1] That comment was made in 1926 and no serious threat to that view has appeared until recently.

But the time is ripe for a revised concept of sentencing, and the suggestion is given here that first we offer the court a much wider choice of noninstitutional dispositions for criminal cases, and at the same time a much more limited choice of dispositions for institu-

[1] Charles E. Vasaly, 56th Annual Congress, American Prison Association, Proceedings, 1926, p. 76.

tional commitments. In fact, the plan being suggested here would include just two general types of institutional commitments and the criteria for these would be quite narrow and specific. Neither one would incorporate the usual feature of indeterminate sentences, the stated minimum time to be served, and a stated maximum, with the parole board having authority to release the inmate when it chooses within those limits.

The approach outlined here does not include all the necessary legal trimmings nor a handy how-to kit for its practical implementation. It is given here only with sufficient form and substance to be a starting point for any legislative reformers who might care to utilize something of its basic principles in shaping future statutes.

In this sentencing model one of the two choices might be called the *specific purpose* sentence. It is intended as a last resort, saved only for those very few offenders who cannot be handled in the community with any of the kinds of resources which we are capable of developing if we want to. This sentence would be indeterminate only in the sense that it would always be imposed for the statutory maximum; the prisoner would be subject to earlier release through *judicial* review, which would be required annually.

Both in its original imposition and in its continuance this sentence must be defensible on highly specific grounds. For instance, the judge may see an offender as a persistent threat who needs psychiatric or other clinical study and treatment which he simply will not get unless they are given in a custodial setting where meanwhile he can be controlled. Or the court may feel that until the defendant receives such corrective help he is too dangerous to live in the community. There may be a health problem, a marital problem, a vocational problem which the judge perceives as basic to the criminal tendencies and he may see the prison as the only feasible place where the corrective help will in fact have a chance to be effective. Accordingly, he could sentence the offender to prison for such specified reasons and for whatever period of time the statute would allow and the treatment plan would require.

This may appear no different from what now happens every day. Perhaps; but there would indeed be one big difference. Under this proposal the judge would be required to state with clarity exactly what problem of the offender is pertinent and exactly what corrective help should be sought. If the prisoner could show that the alleged personal problem is not truly present or if the receiving institution is not actually competent to offer the specified corrective services, he then would have clear grounds to be granted immediate release. No longer could any court sentence a person to an institution with the casual intent that he receive "good discipline," "psychiatric attention," "counseling," "trade training," etc., unless the defendant does need to receive an identified kind of help in a custodial setting and unless such treatment is in true fact adequately rendered in the institution.[2]

Obviously this type of sentence should be used less and less as community-based services gradually develop more specialized capability to provide the needed treatment to such clients without recourse to custody.

Incarceration would be justified under this type of sentence in some cases wherein treatment is not the issue. These would involve offenders who, by some to be developed legal process, are identified as too dangerous to be at large: the cases in which long-time human storage is the only practical means of protecting the public. Here again the court would be required to state this reason clearly and defend it through such exacting measures as the statute would define. Such a sentence should be limited to persons who are dangerous to other people rather than including those who are only property offenders, and here too the continued incarceration would need to be defended on the basis of a periodic and professional appraisal of probable dangerousness.

As already mentioned, a prisoner under the specific purpose sentence could achieve his release when he could convince the sentencing court that the specified reasons for his incarceration have been satisfied. To make sure that the indigent and unsophisticated

[2] The right to treatment is an emerging concept that is taking hold increasingly in respect to commitments to mental hospitals, and its eventual applicability to the corrections field seems safely predictable. For cases on mental commitment see, Rouse v. Cameron, 373, F2d, 451 (D.C. Cir. 1964); Wyatt v. Stickney, 325 F. Supp. 781 (M.D. Ala. 1971).

prisoner does not get lost in this situation the statute would provide for judicial review, again by the sentencing court (or perhaps by a designated court in convenient proximity to the institution), at least annually. Thus, every release from such a prison sentence would be by decision of the same court which originally handed down the sentence in the case and not by a parole board.[3]

The other type of institutional commitment would be the *punishment* sentence, which is offered in frank recognition of the reality of public insistence on punishment.

This is not said without considerable pain in the saying. When our society eventually comes closer to being truly civilized, one of the most salient indices of its progress will be its rejection of punishment as an instrument of criminal justice. However, there are some situations, involving some types of offenders, wherein punishment of a certain quality and brief duration can be truly corrective in its effect.[4] But such cases must be determined on the basis of individualized and clinical analysis rather than on the basis of gross statutory categories as we do now. Punishment has no utility as it is presently applied in the correctional system, but it persists as a strong emotional public need which cannot yet be successfully defied. Though we are still unable to forgo our reliance on punishment, our straining toward a more civilized condition is shown by our effort to fuse treatment with punishment; to assuage our guilt about the revenge motive behind imprisonment by seasoning prison life with rehabilitative services.

In this way we remain confused about the purpose of prison and we provide to our offenders a muddled experience that does not truly help anyone. Reflecting the general ambivalence of society, the custodians are unable to administer with certainty between the incompatible demands of maintaining punitive custody and offering corrective help.

So it will be better when we can renounce punishment as a part

[3] Release by the sentencing court is standard procedure in Denmark where there is no parole board.

[4] Paul W. Keve, "Jail Can Be Useful," *N.P.P.A. News*, vol. 35, no. 5 (November 1956), p. 1.

of the process; but the hard reality is that society is not ready to do so. Accordingly, it would be well for us now to admit that punishment is part of our motive and to provide short fixed sentences for this purpose. Short, because the long sentence is destructive in its effect upon prisoners and it defeats any worthwhile intent. Fixed, because the prisoner is entitled to know what to expect and not to have a discretionary board tinkering with his freedom according to its biases.

The punishment sentence would be very short, certainly no more than six months as an arbitrary and absolute statutory limit. Under such a sentence, stated clearly as intended for punishment, the prisoner would not necessarily be entitled to rehabilitative services as he would be with a special purpose sentence. Actually, however, a fine variety of helping services should be offered, and if they are of genuine merit they will be utilized. But the absence of such services would not be a basis for contesting this type of sentence.

The shortness of the sentence would have real utility. Instead of reducing what the public likes to think of as its protection, the short sentence should have the effect of augmenting it. When sentences are long and severe they are much more hotly contested. The result is that fewer offenders are convicted and for those who are, the costs of prosecution are higher. To handle the increased legal work this makes, the courts and prosecutors must resort to extensive plea bargaining which dilutes the effect and the prestige of the law.

If prosecutors were to bring a great percentage of felony offenders to trial only for punishment sentences of six months or less there would be more convictions, accomplished with less time and cost, and because of the rapid turnover in the resultant institution population, the institutions could be smaller and cheaper. And while the offender is serving his few weeks or months, the fixed time of release obviates the need for him to fake improvement in order to obtain release; he will be less of an escape risk; and the institution can operate with less tension and danger.

To exploit the opportunity for rehabilitative effect, this short-term prisoner should be offered counseling which would study his problem and suggest to him the best ways of dealing with it. The short incarceration provides the chance to diagnose vocational aptitudes and start some training in new job skills. The inside time can then be followed by a period of outside supervision during which the appropriate community resources are enlisted to follow through on the start made in the institution.

In this situation the prisoner has the right not to use the counseling; his only requirement is to serve the specified time. But if the helping services offered are relevant, most prisoners will use them, and they will use them much more sincerely if it has nothing to do with determining the release date.

This is admittedly a bare outline of a sentencing model, which leaves many details and problems unsolved. But the intent here is only to argue a basic principle which would have to be adapted to the needs of each individual state. The greater concern of this chapter is with the alternatives to incarceration.

Financial Sharing

A major effort that must be made in developing alternatives to prisons involves the redesigning of the financial support for correctional programs. The argument has been reiterated over the years that probation should be used more heavily because it costs only pennies per day to supervise a man or woman on probation whereas it costs dollars per day to support the same person in a prison. No matter how valid the argument is, it has little persuasive effect upon the local judge. If he puts the offender in prison it is more costly, to be sure, but the cost is a burden on the *state* (which runs the prison) whereas probation is more often a *county* burden and so the cheaper alternative of probation is no direct saving to the local taxpayers. The economic argument will never be persuasive until state governments at least share with the counties some of the state funds that are saved by community-based local programs used in lieu of state prisons. In fact, California has proved in recent years that an enormous shift away from institutions can be accomplished if the system is rigged not just to equalize or share costs, but to provide impressive economic reward to the counties for handling criminal problems at home.

In 1966 California started its now famous probation subsidy in which cash payments are made to the counties for support of intensive probation and related efforts so that both adult and juvenile offenders can be dealt with at home instead of being committed to state institutions. The effective ingredient in the program is not just money but the fact that the money is paid only on the basis of documented reduction in commitments. The result has been substantially increased capability of probation services (caseloads of 30 to 50 as contrasted with presubsidy caseloads typically of 150 or more), a big increase in the percentage of cases sentenced to probation, and a commensurate decrease in sentences to prisons.

In 1965, 23.3 percent of convicted superior court defendants were sent to California prisons. By 1969 this figure had dropped by 9.8 percent. During the same three-year period the superior court probation caseload increased 53 percent.[5]

During the period from 1966 to 1972, the state of California expended nearly 60 million dollars in subsidy funds, but this was offset by a calculated saving of 186 million dollars gained by closing institutions or canceling plans for others that were to be built.[6]

Toward a Full Measure of Service

Not everyone is convinced of the validity of the California approach but it does make possible a more effective local effort, and sooner or later the correctional services, probably always with state or federal help, must become far more intensive at the local level. No matter how much we learn about good treatment technique, we accomplish little if the caseloads remain too large for proper attention to be given each case. This calls for enunciation of a principle to which government must become committed if we are going to accomplish anything at all in making corrections truly corrective. The simply

[5] Robert L. Smith, A Quiet Revolution, United States Department of Health, Education and Welfare Publication no. (SRS) 72-26011, p. 48.
[6] Ibid., p. 68.

stated principle is that insofar as modern knowledge and skill permits, *help must be given in true proportion to need.*

So far, the instances of this being accomplished are exceedingly rare. Instead we have been doing regularly what we would never condone in the area of medical treatment. It is as if we have a patient whose trouble can be cured by medication which he must take daily, but because of the expense of the medicine the doctor has to divide it among all his patients, permitting each to have a dose about once a week. So the medicine which can cure when given in the proper daily dosage is ineffectual and entirely wasted with only a weekly application.

No doctor would waste his effort in this way, nor would public opinion tolerate such medical practice. Nevertheless, our correctional system has hired some good men and women as probation or parole officers — persons who can be effective in helping maladjusted people — and then has heaped upon them such mountainous caseloads that each client who could have been corrected by daily attention is instead given only fifteen to thirty minutes per month of his agent's time. So the client fails to survive, and because we were unwilling to spend the money to give adequate help in the probation setting where it would have been effective, we return him to prison where the constructive effect is nil and where the daily cost is far more than the cost would have been for intensive probation service.

One of the rare examples of how to give truly adequate attention in a community setting is found in a program known as Home Detention which is an alternative to the usual secure detention for delinquent juveniles awaiting court action. This program, first applied in St. Louis, Missouri, in 1971, has demonstrated that even the impulsive, hostile, persistently delinquent teenager can be stabilized in the community if the service given is commensurate with the needs of the case. In standard juvenile detention practice a boy or girl is detained in secure custody if he or she is considered likely to run away before the case would be heard in court, or if he is likely to commit new delinquencies in the meantime. The test of the Home Detention program then is in whether it can take these young offenders out of custody, put them back on the street, in their homes, and keep them available to the court without new offenses being committed.

Unlike the typical probation program which hires professional personnel and loads them with large numbers of cases, the Home Detention program uses paraprofessional persons and *limits their caseloads to five each.*

Workers are hired without regard to education or experience. Typically the successful person in this job has a high school education or less, is inexperienced in this work but possessed of reasonably good judgment and a genuine liking for youngsters. He is similar to the clientele in race, ethnic origin, and general cultural orientation. He is at home in the same ghettos as his cases.

This worker is hired on a full-time basis and given minimal training, mainly a matter of acquainting him with community resources. Sophisticated training in personality dynamics or casework techniques is deliberately avoided. The job he is given is a stripped down task defined in the most fundamental terms. He is given no office, no desk, no paper work, no set working hours. He is told only that he will have up to five cases at a time and his responsibility is to keep them available to the court and out of trouble. As long as his efforts are ethical, legal, and constructive, he is free to employ any strategy that his own inventiveness may suggest. He is free to work whatever hours he wishes and no one holds him accountable for the amount of time he works. He is free to work when he decides to work and sleep when he decides to sleep. If he can keep his five youngsters stabilized by working an hour or two per day, that is entirely acceptable. He is not paid for putting in time.

What actually happens under such an arrangement? What happens is that the workers become exceedingly challenged by the job and by the flattering latitude they are given to use their own judgment. The freedom from time and paper work requirements is a highly positive morale factor. Instead of skimping on the time given to the job, the workers spend far more time than forty-hour-per-week public servants usually give. They see their clients and their families daily. They remain always in close touch with schoolteachers, employers, parents, police. They are subject to call and quickly responsive twenty-four hours a day. At the juvenile court there is a telephone station where a log is kept of the whereabouts of all the workers all the time so that any worker can be reached within an hour when needed.

Typically, the families from which these delinquents come are multi-problem families, and sometimes because of their limited ability to cope, the problems may be ordinary in quality but frustrating and overwhelming to socially unskilled parents. The children in such a family are sensitive barometers of the family troubles and commonly the child's delinquent behavior can be ameliorated only if the whole family is aided. This has been amply demonstrated by the workers in the Home Detention program who find it necessary constantly to give the most practical and immediate kinds of help. A worker has been known to baby-sit with the several children in a family for two or three days while the mother goes to the hospital; or on finding a family with two of the children ill in a house with electricity and water cut off, the worker has quickly made the necessary contacts to get bills paid and services restored.

These measures are not directly related to correcting a delinquent boy, but they are part of the reason for the effectiveness of the program. When a person of the same culture as the client is able to give immediate problem-solving help without bureaucratic procedures or delays, a feeling of trust rapidly develops and this then is a worker that the family, and the problem child, will use for help with other problems too.

The pertinence of such a program to prison problems may not be immediately apparent for it is aimed at diverting juveniles from detention instead of adults from prison. But it does in fact have relevance because the principle it is demonstrating with juveniles is also adaptable to work with adults. Furthermore, the adult prisoner of ten and twenty years hence is the juvenile who today is being locked in a detention home or the juvenile ward of a jail. By turning a jail key behind a youngster we say to his impressionable mind that he is obviously bad and that the community wishes to be rid of him.

We lessen his self-esteem and therefore his motivation to succeed in nondelinquent living.

For many delinquent careers juvenile detention is the entry point to the criminal justice system, and so it may be fought. Recent federal efforts to make specific immediate reductions in specific crimes are severely handicapped by the political necessity to show demonstrable results *now*. Such efforts should not exactly be discouraged, but the crime problem will not be properly attacked until we put as much effort into reducing *future* crime by interrupting criminal careers at their earliest point of inception.

A wry bit of irony in this is that we will be able to do the more effective job with delinquent juveniles at less cost than we now have with our ineffective methods. The use of "home detention" workers with caseloads of only five each, or the use of probation officers with caseloads of a dozen or less, sounds exceedingly expensive in contrast to typical probation caseloads of fifty to one hundred. But the alternative is the detention home or the state training school where the staff-to-child ratio is more usually one to three and in addition to this tremendous salary cost the institution has the extra burden of housing, feeding, and clothing its inmates. The result is that institutional care is three to four times more expensive than even the super intensive caseloads in the community.

Probation Variations

Especially in the misdemeanor area where the volume of cases is exceedingly high, it is possible for an imaginative court and community to develop, without severe cost, alternatives that are far more constructive than putting offenders in the debilitating care of the typical jail or workhouse. Some of these possibilities are listed below and then discussed in more detail.

1. Suspended sentence without supervision.
2. Fines.
3. Restitutional arrangements — both financial and service.
4. Regular probation with variable approaches.
5. Preincarceration halfway residences.

1. The suspended sentence without supervision is already used extensively but usually under the pretense of regular probation. That is, in any probation caseload of over thirty cases or so certain ones are getting so little supervision as to be only a pretense. It does not matter that the probation officer insists that he sees each case once a month. The fact remains that if a probation client does need restraint and help to remain law abiding, the few minutes of attention that he receives monthly cannot be hoped to counteract the pressures that work against him all the rest of the month. Conversely, if the client does survive through such a probation experience, it clearly means in most cases that he was one of those who was going to make it anyway.

Judges and probation officers cling tenaciously to the hope and belief that even a little probation attention will be of some value, but this ignores the deleterious effect of any process that is not truly honest. While the court may be shocked to hear that its action is not entirely honest, the fact must be faced that the important issue is not what is honest in the mind of the officials, but what is honest as perceived by the person who is to be affected by the process — the client. When an offender is put either on probation or on parole and told that he must obey certain rules and that he will be supervised, and when he quickly realizes that those rules are essentially unenforceable and that supervision is so meager that it is a pretense, he does indeed see the whole thing as hollow, and we are quite defeated in our wish to encourage in him a respect for the law and its enforcement agents.

The solution to this problem is quite simple in concept if not in implementation. We need to sift out the great number of offenders who are not dangerous and whose problem behavior is likely to remain within tolerable limits even when they are provided no official control or help. These can simply be given suspended sentences. It is a matter of saying to the defendant in all honesty, "You are on your own to live as you wish, but if you are rearrested this court may at its discretion invoke the sentence which is now suspended and impose it in addition to any new sentence."

This not only keeps the system honest but it also can help to relieve the heavy probation caseloads so that those who do need real help will have a better chance to get it.

2. Fines are in a category that is included here with reluctance because they can be as counterproductive in some cases as prison itself. Fines often cripple the persons they are intended to correct. The man who lives a marginal existence with barely enough capability to support his family is also likely to be the kind who makes mistakes in judgment that get him into trouble. True enough a fine will be a better alternative than jail, but what he really needs is some *help* — not a financial spanking. The fine succeeds mainly in penalizing his wife and children whose care may require every penny of the family's limited income.

But what of the affluent offender who can easily afford to pay a fine? It may be just as inappropriate there, but for a different reason. The person who can easily afford a fine is hardly impressed by it.

There will be left a limited number of defendants for whom fines will be appropriate but these will be highly individual cases, impossible to categorize, and subject to sensitive selection by the court. Especially to be avoided is the routine imposition of standard fines for specified offenses. This sort of policy has considerable appeal for some courts, but it negates completely the individualized justice that should be the court's pride. There would be more justice in imposing fines of a specified number of days of the defendant's income.

3. It is common enough for restitution to be ordered in cases where a complainant has suffered financial loss. There seems no special need to discuss this concept here. What is yet to be developed is the idea of restitutional service, an idea that has excellent potential but which has had only the barest beginning of a trial.

One court that has used this approach at the misdemeanor level is the municipal court in Royal Oak, Michigan, where in certain cases the defendant is ordered to work for the city for a prescribed number of Saturdays.[7] The idea has also been used in a few juvenile courts.

Altogether, the idea of requiring a defendant to work a number of unpaid hours in some service capacity has tremendous potential. For instance, the affluent but careless person who is convicted of drunk driving — perhaps with consequent damage to persons or property — is not affected much by a fine and may be just as unaffected by anything a probation officer might do for him. But several weekends of required service in a hospital, for example, may be of some actual therapy to him and will be far more in the interests of the taxpayers than supporting him in an expensive jail or prison.

Nor is the idea just for the affluent. It may be even more useful for the marginal person of low social competence. Such a person may have poor self-esteem and little knowledge of some of the social institutions that serve his community. For him there may be therapy in learning that he can give his community real service in some special assignment, and so repay the community for the irritation and expense he has caused it through his offense.

This kind of approach needs to be organized and structured a bit rather than left to the whim of the judge to think of something in each individual case. In an urban court with a substantial volume of cases, the probation service should include a staff person who specializes in providing restitutional services outside the regular probation process. As one illustration of the many possibilities, he could have a regular working arrangement with a nearby mental ' hospital where he could assign offenders under court order to work on weekends or evenings. Regularly assigned hospital staff would supervise such persons in any of the kinds of work commonly given to volunteers, some of it in direct service to patients. As a continuing arrangement the hospital would provide a brief report to the court at the conclusion of each defendant's period of service. The court or probation staff member responsible for administering this restitutional program would maintain several arrangements for dif-

[7] Keve, *Imaginative Programming in Probation and Parole*, p. 263.

ferent types of work in order to meet the varied needs of the clientele. Parks, municipal buildings, housing projects, nursing homes, and community centers are all potential sites for restitutional work programs. The total effect is to provide "punishment" of a most constructive kind and at the same time actual service to the taxpayers that more than offsets the modest cost.

4. Regular probation needs sprucing up with new techniques of caseload management which might give the old probation process a fresh effectiveness. Altogether, this can by itself be the subject of a book; here it can only be suggested what some of the possibilities are.

Techniques of more efficient caseload management have been developed in recent years but are so far used only in occasional instances. The idea of caseload management includes a number of variations on the usual probation or parole practice, adapting the helping process to local conditions, to different types of clients, to the varying degrees of intensity needed, and to diverse kinds of personnel. In large cities where there is a steady high volume of cases, this can mean developing specialized caseloads that serve such types as drug users, alcoholics, career criminals, clients with low intelligence, and mentally gifted clients.

Whether or not specialization of this sort is tried, the professional probation officer must become a team leader. He might continue to have forty to sixty cases, but he will share the work with at least half a dozen auxiliary people. Two or three of them will be the same free-roving indigenous workers as are used in the Home Detention program, taking the most volatile cases of the moment and giving them maximum daily attention as long as it is needed. The other auxiliary persons may be trainees or case aides, who are less qualified, but are constantly available to help with all the practical problem-solving matters that are so important in enabling the typical client to remain stable. As an example, the Oregon Division of Corrections has introduced into its Portland office a team concept in which each probation or parole officer may carry a fairly large caseload, but is aided by up to six persons variously classified as aides or trainees, although they may be volunteers or students. The team approach, with the help of these less expensive people, increases the agency's capacity to be responsive to problems at all hours, a most important consideration since the crises that need immediate attention are not likely to occur during conventional office hours. The plan also makes available to each case the varied talents, ideas, and capabilities of these several workers.

A most basic principle of the whole probation effort, whatever the approach, is that each case must be individualized much more than is common so far. Probation officers like to think that they are in the business of giving individualized treatment but their work can become too easily institutionalized, especially when caseloads get heavy and contacts with clients must be regimented. The staff must evaluate every case individually to determine what help it needs and must arrange for or give that help fully, without being tied to any standard or routine probation practices that are not entirely defensible in respect to that particular client's own needs.

A probation officer will in all his cases be alert to the possibility of utilizing special community resources. He may do his best work when he gets someone else to do his work for him. In fact, there may be one special variation of probation that utilizes this notion as its central method. This would involve cases which from the beginning are to be on conventional probation supervision for three months or less, after which supervision and assistance would be given by a volunteer or some other community agency.

This plan would be based on the assumption that many clients need help mostly in the first few days or weeks of probation and also that the help needed in many cases is available from other resources in the community. The purpose would be to provide intensive help in the beginning and at the same time to pursue quite aggressively the acquisition of some special resource which could give the client continuing help.

Because this continuing help could be offered by an active volunteer program, a big part of the work during the first few weeks would be to select and introduce a volunteer to the case. Once a viable linkup is accomplished, the probation officer could cease his activity, leaving the case to the volunteer. In itself this is not so new, but too often the volunteer, left to himself, is not dependably persistent over the long haul. To ensure effective follow-through, a well-trained secretary should have responsibility for calling each volunteer monthly on a regular schedule to check the case progress. If she detects any danger signals or any lapse of the volunteer's service, she can alert the probation officer, who then would proceed to see what problem may need attention. If necessary, he could then resume his activity in the case, but at least this routine check-up will serve to alert the volunteer to his responsibility and assure him that the probation agency is serious in its expectations.

For those cases which the probation officer himself keeps and works with there needs to be a wider variety of approaches than the standard one-to-one counseling with routine reporting to the proba-tion office. The development of a team of auxiliary staff to aid the probation officer will make possible such devices as group counsel-ing or special groups to deal with special problems. In a dynamic probation service these varying treatment approaches would come and go according to the needs of the caseload. Too often we find it difficult to give up a particular method, procedure, or program for this may imply that it was not good. Instead we must recognize that there is less virtue in permanence than in adapting to the demands of the moment.

A grossly neglected source of help for the probation clientele is the clientele itself. In every large probation caseload there is certain to be one or several persons who have truly improved and stabilized. These represent a vital source of especially effective help if they are properly used. Such a person, in his last six months under supervision, could be told that his final requirement as a pro-bationer is to take responsibility for helping other probationers who need the kind of guidance he can give. The artistry in this is to use these advanced probationers in various individualized assignments appropriate to their abilities. In a large probation office they may even be organized into a group that meets both to obtain guidance from staff and to feed back to staff their own sharp brand of advice. Such a process can serve not only to provide extra helpers to the probation staff but also to keep it sensitized to the real feelings of the clientele.

5. Residential probation began about 1950 in this country with the appearance of halfway houses. Soon these residential facilities began to appear in most states and in rich variety. So far they have been mainly for persons leaving prison who need an intermediary shelter while getting reestablished in the community, but there finally is the beginning of a trend to develop these residences as substitutes for the prison. In this sense they become halfway *in* residences instead of the halfway *out* facilities as first conceived. Instances of these are few so far, and it is far too soon to expect any demonstrable proof of their utility, but on the basis of all we know about the tragic experience with prisons and about treatment in community settings, it must be assumed that a skillfully operated halfway *in* house can be a vital adjunct to probation and one of the most hopeful alternatives to prison presently known. An excellent example of this concept is a residence called PORT in Rochester, Minnesota.

A small citizen's group in Rochester started this project in 1969 at the urging of the two district court judges. It was housed in an unused building on the grounds of the Rochester State Hospital. Like many such mental hospitals, this one had experienced a reduction in patients and as one result there was a large nurses' residence that was empty, though still in good condition. It was ideal housing for the purpose, for the program benefited from its proximity to the hospital's clinical services and it had the cordial support of the hospital superintendent, a member of the PORT Board.

This program is not for just any probationer, for the court is conscientious in referring to PORT only those serious cases that would otherwise be certain to go to prison. The real purpose of the program would have been defeated if it had been used as a substitute for probation rather than for prison. An intake committee from the PORT Board assists the court in screening the cases for admission. As an important part of the admission process, the defendant lives at PORT for two or three weeks pending court disposition of his case and final decision on his admission. If the decision is for him to go to PORT instead of to prison, he is placed on probation on condition that he live at the PORT residence until released by a joint decision of staff and court.

Like in a work-release situation, the PORT residents maintain regular jobs and go to work daily. They are expected to return to the residence promptly after work and all activity in nonworking hours is subject to house rules.

PORT is far more than a residence with control, since it is assumed that every resident seriously needs help in learning how to live more successfully. The staff consists of a director and assistant director, both professionally trained in social work and both experienced in other correctional settings. These two and a secretary are the basic staff, but they are significantly augmented by various other persons, especially several college students.

The probationer residents, anywhere from twenty to twenty-five of them, live in the rooms formerly housing nurses, and interspersed among them are students who also live there and participate in the program. This is a vital ingredient from the standpoint of reducing the stigmatic quality that a residence gets when it serves offenders exclusively. At the same time, the students can help the treatment process in different ways. Because they live in, which the professional does not, they mix with the probationers daily in the activities of ordinary living. A conversation while shaving together in a common bathroom, for instance, is a casual, nonthreatening encounter which becomes a new and especially useful kind of relationship for the probationer. The students are expected to mix freely with the probationers in a simple person-to-person manner and to utilize in a natural way any openings they find for being of help. They serve as a model to the probationers, and are useful for this purpose even if the model is a bit blemished at times. If one of the students slips and is brought home drunk on a Saturday night, for instance, it is not the cause for dismay that would have brought quick dismissal from earlier programs where the only allowable model was strictly sober rectitude. Instead, here is an opportunity for both students and probationers to examine the episode in a group session the next day. It is a chance for the probationers to analyze why it is that this person can drink without consequent criminal behavior while they so often conclude a drinking spree in jail with new charges to face.

In any event, the introduction of student residents makes the setting a more natural one; it augments the capabilities of the staff since the students take turns in being responsible for the house on assigned nights and weekends; and it provides a training experience to supplement the studies of those students in the social sciences. Students receive their board and room without charge, but no cash salary.

The major active ingredients in the treatment process at PORT are the frequent group sessions and a system of progress through levels of privilege. The group meetings are held at least four scheduled times per week and more often if specific needs arise. These are intensive encounters in which the emphasis is on a ruthlessly honest examination of any person's problem behavior in an attempt to help him understand and overcome it.

The other treatment element, a type of behavior modification process, is the requirement that the resident earn his way to increased privileges and eventually to release. For instance, the new resident may leave the building only in the company of a counselor except when going to work or school; he may go out with his parents only with staff or group permission.

Gradually the resident may gain more privileges by accumulating points for consistently good work on the job or in school, for holding to schedules, for keeping his room in good order, for maintaining good appearance, and for reliable handling of his funds. Furthermore, this outward behavior must be convincingly bolstered by his attitude which his peers will assess quite perceptively in the group meetings.

Demotion to a state of lesser privilege is always a possibility too when irresponsible behavior occurs. But whether the progress is forward or backward, the residents as a group are given the responsibility for each decision as far as possible. The principle employed here is the same as that mentioned in the previous discussion of inmate councils. The staff does not surrender its authority; the group is well aware that the staff reserves the right to make all final decisions. But the staff recognizes that the clientele must learn, above all else, to exercise responsibility, and this calls for daily practice in arriving at responsible decisions. So the group focuses its daily discussions on issues of personal behavior, how to improve it, and what rewards or sanctions should be related to it.

There is one feature of the PORT program that is unorthodox enough to dismay anyone who is strongly committed to the conventional separation of juvenile and adult offenders. The program accepts both and maintains a careful balance of juveniles and young adults. The experience makes us stop and reconsider the reasons why we have always been so adamant about separating adults and juveniles. The principle was developed in the context of the jail where offenders sit around in unprogrammed, debilitating storage. In that situation certainly there is good reason for not mixing less sophisticated persons, whatever their age, with more degenerate offenders.

But a program like PORT is altogether different from the custodial jail or prison. PORT, because of its openness, its community setting, and its college student residents, is less stigmatic than even the conventional training schools for juveniles; and, most important, it brings people together in a dynamic relationship wherein a persistent and pervasive attitude of concern is uppermost. In the context of the jail, prisoners will tend to relate at the level of the worst aspects of their personalities. But in a skillfully directed therapeutic setting such as PORT, the residents find themselves developing their better qualities in dealing with one another. For instance, one of the boys, having trouble with schoolwork, is tutored by one of the adults who finds his own sense of self-worth enhanced by his being able to help another. The adults in turn may be prodded into greater effort to progress through the levels of privilege when they see the more adaptive youngsters surpassing them. The fact is that in this kind of environment there is no problem of the adult criminalizing the juvenile, but instead a vital and healthy concern for each other develops.

One more essential point: the community is involved. Despite current and spotty attempts to get lay citizens active in some of the prison programs, there is something inherent in the traditional prison that tends to keep outsiders at arm's length. But the PORT program and its surrounding community reach out to each other, and their interaction is a vital ingredient in the program's functioning. The board itself is composed of people who represent both the lay power structure of the community and all components of the criminal justice system. More importantly, they are put to work. They serve seriously on subcommittees that deal with the screening of new residents and their education and employment; and they help with decisions about the program, administration, and personnel policies of the residence.

To widen citizen involvement, the residence holds open houses and organizes the participation of a number of volunteers. Not only PORT, but many other community-based programs have found that this cordially aggressive involvement of the citizenry is the key to community toleration as well as an indispensable source of strength.

But Where Is Deterrence?

The instinctive public reaction to even the best concepts of noninstitutional measures is to wonder what deterrent effect will be left. The natural, human, and urgent feeling is that there still must be a big stick somewhere, a period of lockup in unpleasant conditions, or else crime will be uncontrolled.

Hard as it is to believe, however, most offenders do not turn to criminal activity as a first choice — whether or not punishment may be in the offing. Deterrence is not inherent in the threat of prison. [Deterrence is a matter of providing alternative opportunities that are meaningful and satisfying.]

It is as simple as that, and as dreadfully difficult as that. But it is only in that direction that any true resolution of the crime control problem will eventually be found.

The common problem, yours, mine, everyone's,
Is not to fancy what were fair in life
Provided it could be, — but, finding first
What may be, then find how to make it fair
Up to our means: a very different thing!

from "Bishop Blougram's Apology"
by Robert Browning

Selected Bibliography

Selected Bibliography

The Historical Prison

Carleton, Mark T. *Politics and Punishment: A History of the Louisiana State Penal System.* Baton Rouge: Louisiana State University Press, 1971.

Grunhut, Max. *Penal Reform: A Comparative Study.* Montclair, N.J.: Patterson Smith, 1948.

Hibbert, Christopher. *The Roots of Evil: A Social History of Crime and Punishment.* Boston: Little, Brown, 1963.

Lewis, O. F. *The Development of American Prisons and Prison Customs.* New York: Prison Association of New York, 1922.

McKelvey, Blake. *American Prisons.* Chicago: University of Chicago Press, 1936.

Rothman, David. *Discovery of the Asylum.* Boston: Little, Brown, 1971.

Teeters, Negley K. *The Cradle of the Penitentiary.* Philadelphia: Temple University, sponsored by the Pennsylvania Prison Society, 1955.

Prison in the Perspective of the Criminal Justice System

American Friends Service Committee. *Struggle for Justice: A Report on Crime and Punishment in America.* New York: Hill and Wang, 1971.

Clark, Ramsey. *Crime in America.* New York: Simon and Schuster, 1970.

Fox, Vernon. *Introduction to Corrections.* Englewood Cliffs, N.J.: Prentice-Hall, 1972.

Goldfarb, Ronald L., and Linda R. Singer. *After Conviction.* New York: Simon and Schuster, 1973.

Grupp, Stanley, ed. *Theories of Punishment.* Bloomington: Indiana University Press, 1971.

Menninger, Karl. *The Crime of Punishment.* New York: Viking Press, 1968.

National Advisory Commission on Criminal Justice Standards and Goals. *The Report on Corrections.* Washington, D.C., 1973.

Ohlin, Lloyd E., ed. *Prisoners in America.* Englewood Cliffs, N.J.: Prentice-Hall, 1973.
Perlman, Harvey S., and Thomas B. Allington, eds. *The Tasks of Penology.* Lincoln: University of Nebraska Press, 1969.
Shaw, George Bernard. *The Crime of Imprisonment.* New York: Greenwood Press, 1946.

Analysis of Prison Life and Management

American Bar Association, Resource Center on Correctional Law and Legal Services, and the American Correctional Association. *Legal Responsibility and Authority of Correctional Officers.* Washington, D.C., 1974.
Carter, Robert M., Daniel Glaser, and Leslie T. Wilkins. *Correctional Institutions.* New York: J. B. Lippincott, 1972.
Clemmer, Donald. *The Prison Community.* New York: Rinehart, 1958.
Cressey, Donald R., ed. *The Prison: Studies in Institutional Organization and Change.* New York: Holt, Rinehart and Winston, 1961.
deFord, Miriam Allen. *Stone Walls.* Philadelphia and New York: Chilton, 1962.
Glaser, Daniel. *The Effectiveness of a Prison and Parole System.* Indianapolis: Bobbs-Merrill, 1964.
Goffman, Erving. *Asylums.* Chicago: Aldine, 1962.
Hopper, Columbus B. *Sex in Prison: The Mississippi Experiment with Conjugal Visiting.* Baton Rouge: Louisiana State University Press, 1969.
Johnston, Norman. *The Human Cage.* Philadelphia: Published for the American Foundation Institute of Correction, by Walker, New York, 1973.
Lindner, Robert M. *Stone Walls and Men.* New York: Odyssey Press, 1946.
Mitford, Jessica. *Kind and Usual Punishment.* New York: Alfred A. Knopf, 1973.
Nagel, William G. *The New Red Barn.* Philadelphia: Published for the American Foundation Institute of Correction, by Walker, New York, 1973.
Parker, Tony. *The Frying Pan.* New York: Basic Books, 1970.
Scudder, Kenyon. *Prisoners Are People.* Garden City, N.Y.: Doubleday, 1952.
South Carolina Department of Corrections, Collective Violence Research Project. *Collective Violence in Correctional Institutions: A Search for Causes.* Columbia, 1973.
Sykes, Gresham M. *The Society of Captives.* Princeton, N.J.: Princeton University Press, 1958.
Ward, David A., and Gene C. Kassebaum. *Women's Prison.* Chicago: Aldine, 1965.
Wilkinson, Fred T. *The Realities of Crime and Punishment.* Springfield, Mo.: Mycroft Press, 1972.

The Offender

Deutsch, Martin, Irwin Katz, and Arthur R. Jensen. *Social Class, Race and Psychological Development.* New York: Holt, Rinehart and Winston, 1968.
Gaddis, Thomas E., and James O. Long. *Killer.* New York: Macmillan, 1970.

The Inmate View

Cleaver, Eldridge. *Soul on Ice.* New York: Dell, 1968.
Harrison, Eddie, and Alfred V. J. Prather. *No Time for Dying.* Englewood Cliffs, N.J.: Prentice-Hall, 1973.
Irwin, John. *The Felon.* Englewood Cliffs, N.J.: Prentice-Hall, 1970.
Johnson, Lester Douglas. *The Devil's Front Porch.* Lawrence: University Press of Kansas, 1970.

Laite, W. E., Jr. *The United States vs. William Laite.* Washington, D.C.: Acropolis Books, 1972.

Levy, Howard, and David Miller. *Going to Jail.* New York: Grove Press, 1971.

Martin, John Bartlow. *My Life in Crime: The Autobiography of a Professional Criminal.* New York: Harper & Brothers, 1952.

Minton, Robert J., Jr., ed. *Inside: Prison American Style.* New York: Random House, 1971.

Serge, Victor. *Men in Prison.* Garden City, N.Y.: Doubleday, 1969.

The Roots of Disturbance

Attica. The official report of the New York State Special Commission on Attica. New York: Bantam Books, 1972.

McGraw, Peg, and Walter McGraw. *Assignment: Prison Riots.* New York: Henry Holt, 1954.

South Carolina Department of Corrections, Collective Violence Research Project. *Collective Violence in Correctional Institutions: A Search for Causes.* Columbia, 1973.

Alternatives

Fenton, Norman. *Explorations in the Use of Group Counseling in the County Correctional Program.* Palo Alto, Calif.: Pacific Books, 1962.

Glasser, William. *Reality Therapy.* New York: Harper and Row, 1965.

Kassebaum, Gene, David A. Ward, and Daniel M. Wilner. *Prison Treatment and Parole Survival.* New York: John Wiley, 1971.

Keve, Paul W. *Imaginative Programming in Probation and Parole.* Minneapolis: University of Minnesota Press, 1967.

————. *Prison, Probation or Parole?* Minneapolis: University of Minnesota Press, 1954.

Morris, Norval, and Gordon Hawkins. *The Honest Politician's Guide to Crime Control.* Chicago: University of Chicago Press, 1969.

National Probation Association. *John Augustus, First Probation Officer.* New York, 1939.

Index

Index